Insights into the Unknown
A Ghost Hunter's Journey

Copyright © 2015 Greg Feketik

ALL RIGHTS RESERVED

Greg Feketik

gefeketik@gmail.com

www.tcghohio.org

Edited by Shannon Dillon

Printed by CreateSpace, an Amazon.com Company

This book is dedicated to my loving parents George and Arlene Feketik who taught me right from wrong. They were very interested and supportive in my paranormal endeavors. I am the person I am today because of them. They are both in a better place now, and finally have the answers to all of life's mysteries.

I would like to thank all my friends and family who helped me by reading the rough draft of this book, and giving me suggestions and ideas on content and grammar.

Special thanks to my wife Kathy, who, without her love and support, this book would have never happened. I am sorry for making you read it multiple times, and for all of the hours I had to spend on my computer writing and rewriting, but at least you were able to watch *your* favorite television shows in peace!

TABLE OF CONTENTS

INTRODUCTION

Do you believe in ghosts? Did you know that almost half of all Americans do?

I have been researching and investigating the paranormal for many years, and I still don't have all the answers and I probably never will. In fact I don't believe anyone ever will. I am still searching for the *"Insights into the Unknown."* Insight means the ability to understand people and situations in a very clear way; an understanding of the true nature of something. The *Merriam-Webster Dictionary* defines unknown as a place, situation, or thing that you do not know about or understand or something that is not known or not yet discovered.

I remember when death entered my life for the first time. It was my seventh birthday party way back in March of 1965. Both of my grandparents came over to our house to celebrate. I remember having a good time. Death was the farthest thing from my mind. The next day, I found out that my mom's father, my grandfather, had passed away during the night in his sleep. But how could that be? He was just with us the evening before and he didn't look or feel sick. Besides, he was only in his forties, a very young man. I remember my mother becoming very upset and my dad trying to comfort her.

Later, after his funeral, we were at his house in Highland Hills, Ohio, where he lived with my grandmother—the same house where he had just passed away. I remember all of the adults standing around talking, and I was just standing there by myself when I looked down the hallway toward the bedroom he died in. Just then, the hallway lights flashed off and on. I figured that was my grandfather saying goodbye and that he was all right.

But do we really know if my grandfather was all right and in a better place? Could there really be life after death or does your whole being, mind and soul, cease to exist? Is it just a blackness like when you're put under anesthesia and before the time you wake up after surgery? I have had numerous surgeries during my lifetime and I have never remembered anything during the time the surgery is occurring. When I woke up, the only thing I remembered was the operating room just prior to going under. How do we find the answers to these questions, especially if one does not have faith?

What is faith? According to the *Merriam-Webster Dictionary*, faith is a firm belief in something for which there is no proof. However, just because someone has a strong belief in something, that does not make it the truth or a scientific fact.

There are a lot of people who believe in ghosts, and there are just as many who do not, and it has nothing to do with religion or faith. Either you believe or you do not.

The people who do not believe in ghosts need tangible proof that something is real. That's where paranormal investigators come in when dealing with ghosts, hauntings and the unknown, the same way cryptozoologists search for unknown animals such as Bigfoot.

One of the reasons I started investigating the paranormal was to prove to myself and others that there is something when we die and that spirits and ghosts can interact with us on our plane.

There is tons of evidence out there pointing to the existence of ghosts, including photographs, audio recordings and video recordings. So why don't people believe in ghosts if there is so much so-called evidence?

I believe there are a couple of reasons. First, the skeptics would have to experience it for themselves, because they will always claim that all of the evidence has logical explanations or the evidence was faked. Secondly, most of the evidence gathered has not been obtained in a scientific manner. May I suggest reading the book, *The Art and Science of Paranormal Investigation* by Jeffrey Dwyer, PH.D[1] for further information on the scientific method of paranormal investigations.

I may not be able to convince a lot of people that ghosts exist, but I wanted to convince myself and that was the main reason I started investigating.

My very first investigation happened in 1991 which I'll talk about in chapter one. In 2005, my wife and I joined a paranormal group in Northeast Ohio. In 2012, seven members of that group left, including myself, and formed Tri-C Ghost Hunters in January of 2013. Now the main reason I investigate is to help others who may be experiencing paranormal phenomenon in their homes or businesses.

This is not a tech book, reference book, travel book or a how-to book. My goal in writing this book isn't to change anyone's beliefs—that is totally up to you. It is a book to let you, the reader, know that there are things that happen in this everyday world that we, as paranormal investigators, cannot explain. Is it paranormal? Is it natural? Is there a logical explanation? The answer to all of these questions is……possibly.

One last thing—all of the stories and incidents you are about to read are 100% true. None of the stories were exaggerated and everything happened exactly as I tell them. All I ask is that you keep an open mind. So far, I have been on over 135 investigations—everything from a small two-bedroom apartment in West Virginia to a large medieval castle in Scotland—so please believe me when I say things really do go bump in the night...Enjoy

CHAPTER ONE

EARLY INFLUENCES:

BIRTH OF A GHOST HUNTER

My interest in the paranormal and the unexplained began in the early 1970s when I was about 13 years old. Mike, my best friend who lived right next door, and I had an "out-of-this-world" experience—or so we thought at the time.

I was living with my parents and younger sister in the Glenwood Acres development, within the Village of Twinsburg, Ohio. Glenwood Acres was built in 1956 and was street upon street of about 400 low-cost, identical, three-bedroom ranch homes with no garages or basements. The development was built in conjunction with the new Chrysler Stamping Plant, which was also being constructed at the same time, to provide housing for the 3,500 workers who would be employed there. The Village of Twinsburg, conveniently located halfway between Cleveland and Akron, had a population of just over 6,000[2] people back then and was mostly country and farms. I think we had one traffic light in the whole village.

Mike, who was the same age as me, and his brother Kenny, who was four years older, delivered the old *Cleveland Press*[3] newspaper at that time. The newspaper shut down in June 1982 after 104 years of publication. Unlike most newspapers today, the *Cleveland Press* newspaper was delivered every evening, except Sunday, when it was delivered in the early morning hours. I used to help Mike and Kenny deliver the papers every Sunday morning. I thought it was cool getting up while it was still dark and riding my bike. I felt on top of the world and didn't mind getting up at 4:00 a.m. I was a working man.

Just like the Sunday newspapers of today, the *Press* Sunday paper was large with a lot of sections that needed to be put together prior to delivery. The newspaper delivery truck would drop the newspapers off around 4:00 a.m. at an intersection about a half-mile from where we lived. We would ride our bicycles up the street in the dark morning hours to pick up the newspapers and bring them back to Mike and Kenny's house. Once back at the house, we would then proceed to put the different sections of the newspapers together. We usually had to make several trips, because we could only carry so many papers in our newspaper bags and we had to deliver to almost the whole neighborhood. It's not like it is today where adults deliver newspapers from their cars, throwing them from their windows while driving down the street. Back then, it was teenage boys riding their bicycles, or walking, delivering the papers to the front door in hopes of earning an extra buck.

On this particular warm and clear summer Sunday morning, we all woke up, hopped on our bikes and pedaled to the pick-up location to gather up all the newspapers. This morning was no different than any other Sunday morning. We rode up our street about a quarter of a mile and then turned right onto another street, where we rode another quarter of a mile to the pick-up location. We arrived at the location and got to work packing up the newspapers when all of a sudden all three of us noticed a bright green ball of light "dancing" in the tree line across the street, north of where we were. The ball of light was a little over a quarter mile away, across an open field and was moving back and forth in a horizontal manner. From our vantage point, it appeared to be about two feet in diameter. It was not huge by any means, but it was big enough and bright enough for all three of us to see it clearly. We all stood there awestruck, wondering what we were seeing. What could this strange ball of light be? Could it be someone carrying a flashlight or a lantern? Why would someone be out this early in the morning walking in the woods? No, that couldn't be it, we quickly decided. But wait, the ball of light seemed to be in the *top* of the trees, going from treetop to treetop! What is that? We probably stood there and watched it for fifteen minutes. We waited to see if it would do anything different, but it just kept bouncing from tree to tree. We wanted to watch it longer, but we knew we had to get the newspapers back to the house for delivery. We packed our newspaper bags with as many papers as we could and rode our bikes back home. Once back at the house, Kenny, being the oldest, told Mike and me to go back and get the rest of the newspapers, so off we went on our bikes for another load, not thinking we would see the ball of light again. When we arrived back at the location, we looked for the green ball of light in the far-off trees, but it was nowhere to be found. Whew! We were glad it went away. It sort of scared us when we first saw it because we didn't know what it was. We proceeded to start loading the papers onto our bikes when out of the corner of our eyes we saw it again! Our jaws dropped and we stood there frozen in fear! The ball of green light was in the ditch, right alongside the road, not 50 feet from where we were standing! We both screamed at the same time, jumped on our bikes and raced for home, pedaling as fast as we could, leaving behind the rest of the papers, and never looking back! We could hardly catch our breath as we excitedly tried to tell Kenny what we had seen. Kenny at this point didn't seem to care about our close call with the supernatural and possible abduction. All he cared about was getting the papers delivered. He told us we had to go back and get the rest. We said, "No way! We're not going back there so that thing can get us!" It was probably a probe from some alien spaceship looking for teenage boys to abduct! "If you're so brave and want to get abducted, you go get the rest of the papers yourself!" we exclaimed. After teenage boy bantering and arguing, we all three decided to return to pick up the rest of the papers. We got on our bikes and reluctantly rode back to the scene. Very timidly we scanned the surrounding roadside where we last saw the ball of light as we all approached the rest of the newspapers, lying there untouched. At least the newspapers weren't "abducted," so that was a good thing. Our muscles tensed and our feet were already facing in the direction of home, ready to flee at a moment's notice. We wanted to make sure the ball of light didn't sneak up on us so Mike and I stood "guard" touching back to back while Kenny loaded up the rest of the papers onto his bike. All three of us then raced back home, pedaling as fast as we could, not looking back or wanting to be the last one home in case the ball was chasing us! You know they always get the slow ones. You don't have to be the fastest, but you sure don't want to be the slowest.

It was a close call, but all three of us survived our first encounter with the unknown that morning. For weeks afterward, we talked about what happened among ourselves and with family and friends. A lot of people thought we were crazy and stated we were just making it up. It didn't matter what other people thought. We knew whatever we encountered was real. We just had to figure out what it was.

Several years later, while reading one of the many books on UFO's, that I loved reading, I discovered what we had probably encountered that morning was a natural phenomenon called "ball lightning."[4] Ball lightning is an unexplained atmospheric electrical phenomenon. The term refers to luminous, usually spherical objects, which vary from pea-sized to almost 10 feet in diameter! It is usually associated with thunderstorms, but lasts considerably longer than the split-second flash of a lightning bolt. At least that is the closest logical explanation I could come up with at the time.

A decade and a half later, in 1987, I had a house built in almost exactly the same location where Mike, Kenny and I first saw that bright green ball of light dancing among the treetops in the early seventies. The strange ball of light was never seen again by any of us. But who knows, maybe another group of teenage boys witnessed the same things during an early morning ride. I wonder if they were as brave as us.

Because of that one experience, I became interested in anything about the unknown and started reading everything I could get my hands on about the subject. One of the first books I read was actually a series of books called *Alfred Hitchcock and The Three Investigators*.[5] For those who may not know, *The Three Investigators* was a juvenile detective series, where teenagers, Jupiter "Jupe" Jones, Peter "Pete" Crenshaw and Robert "Bob" Andrews solved all sorts of intriguing mysteries such as *The Secret of Terror Castle, The Secret of the Haunted Mirror* and my favorite, *The Mystery of the Green Ghost*. Those books got me started. I was hooked! I also started reading the *Hardy Boys Mysteries*[6] about the adventures of Frank and Joe Hardy, who like *The Three Investigators*, were amateur sleuths. I wanted to read every book about unexplained phenomenon I could get my hands on from the local public library. We didn't have the internet back in the seventies when I was a teenager. We had to get all of our information from libraries and encyclopedias, which was a lot harder to do when you had to do a book report for school! I read books about Bigfoot, The Loch Ness Monster, the Abominable Snowman of the Himalayas,

The Bermuda Triangle, ghosts and my favorite, UFO's. I read them all—Hans Holzer, Charles Berltiz, John G. Fuller, and Ed and Lorraine Warren, just to name a few of the authors and researchers who delved into that subject matter.

I would often daydream and plan my trips to Loch Ness near Inverness, Scotland, to look for the Loch Ness Monster. Another friend of mine, also named Mike, and I were going to travel down the darkest Amazon tributaries searching for the "Creature from the Black Lagoon." I thought the creature was real too. Yeah, I know. I wanted to believe it all! We were then going to the Pacific Northwest in search of the elusive Bigfoot. I remember reading about "Momo the Missouri Monster"[7] when it was in all of the papers in the early seventies. Momo was said to be a seven-foot-tall, hairy creature that had a large pumpkin-shaped head and emitted a terrible odor. All of my friends, including both Mikes, and I would sit up in our favorite apple trees in the local apple orchard calling out for Momo to come and get us, "HEY MOHHH MOHHH!" we used to yell.

I wanted to be a famous explorer and adventurer and prove to everyone that these cryptids did exist. Back then I believed with all my heart that they were all real. There were too many reports and witness sightings for them not to be. These witnesses were all seeing something that was unknown to them. Even now, I do believe there is a large humanoid primate living in the Pacific Northwest, commonly known as Bigfoot and Sasquatch, but that story is for another book.

As I got older, I realized that my adventures I once dreamed about were unrealistic. Yet, I did accomplish one of those adventures I used to dream about. In October of 2010, I was finally able to cruise on Loch Ness when my wife Kathy and I traveled to England and Scotland on our vacation that year. We stayed in a haunted castle just outside of Inverness called Castle Stuart, which we had the pleasure of investigating for a couple of nights. We booked an excursion on the Jacobite Cruise Line[8] located in Inverness. We sailed about five and a half miles on The Jacobite Queen down the Caledonian Canal from the Tomnahurich Bridge into Loch Ness. It was a dream come true. Hoping to catch a glimpse of Nessie, I searched high and low while on the canal and the River Ness, which paralleled the canal. Once on the loch, I scanned the horizon, the shoreline and every inch of the loch that I could see with my naked eyes. I watched the sonar they had on the boat, hoping to see something large swim by, but of course it didn't happen. Oh, well, I really didn't think I was going to see her. It is still a magical and beautiful place to visit and I recommend it to anyone visiting Scotland. One adventure down and two to go! I'm still trying to get my wife to travel to the Pacific Northwest to help me search for Bigfoot. We may even try searching for Bigfoot in Southeastern Ohio and Southwestern Pennsylvania, which is closer to where we live. I may have a better chance of being abducted by aliens from outer space than finding a Bigfoot in Ohio. But you never know— anything can happen.

During my teen years I was really hooked on UFO's and the Bermuda Triangle. I remember reading a lot about alien abductions and disappearances in the "Triangle." I was intrigued by The Barney and Betty Hill Case[9] and was baffled by the disappearance of Flight 19[10], which disappeared while flying a training mission through the Triangle.

Barney and Betty Hill (See Figure 1) were an interracially married couple who were allegedly abducted by aliens in September 1961 while travelling in their car near Lancaster, New Hampshire. A book about their abduction, *The Interrupted Journey: Two Lost Hours Aboard a Flying Saucer*, published in 1966, was written by John G. Fuller. A television movie was made in 1975 of the abduction, called *The UFO Incident*, starring James Earl Jones and Estelle Parsons as Barney and Betty Hill. What I found particularly interesting about this case is the "star map" Betty drew while under hypnosis. During a hypnosis session, Betty stated while she was on board the alien

Figure 1 - Betty & Barney Hill

space craft she was shown a star map of a solar system. Some of the stars had heavy solid lines, light solid lines and broken lines connecting them. When she asked what the lines meant, she was told the heavy solid lines were trade routes, the light solid lines were

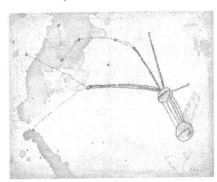

Figure 2 - Betty Hill's original star map

places they traveled to occasionally and the broken lines were expeditions. To this day there is still great controversy about the alleged abduction and the star map.

Researchers are still trying to determine where the stars from the star map are in the solar system (See Figure 2).

One of the most famous and mysterious disappearance of all time in the Bermuda Triangle was the disappearance of Flight 19, which occurred in December 1945. It was so famous that Steven Spielberg

12

incorporated the disappearance of Flight 19 into his 1977 hit movie, *Close Encounters of the Third Kind*. At the beginning of the movie,

all of the missing planes are found intact and operational in the Sonoran Desert – minus any trace of the crew members. The plot indicates that the crew was abducted by aliens and their planes were placed in the desert where they were later

Figure 3 - TBM Avengers similar to the ones missing in Flight 19

found. Near the end of the film, the missing crew members emerge from an alien mothership near Devil's Tower, Wyoming. After being missing for more than 30 years, none of them have aged. Hopefully everyone reading this book has seen the movie and I did not give anything away.

On December 5, 1945 at 2:10 p.m. EST, five United States Navy TBM Avenger torpedo bombers (See Figure 3), along with 14 crewmembers, took off from the Naval Air Station Ft. Lauderdale, Florida on a training mission that took them through the Bermuda Triangle. For reasons unknown, all five planes became lost. The last transmission occurred at 7:04 p.m., when Lt. Charles Taylor, the flight leader, was heard saying, "All planes close up tight... we'll have to ditch unless landfall... when the first plane drops below 10 gallons, we all go down together." A Navy PBM Mariner flying boat (See Figure 4) was sent to search for the missing fliers. It too disappeared without a trace with 13 crew members aboard. To this date, no trace of the six planes or the 27 crew members has ever been found.

Figure 4 - PBM Mariner similar to the one that disappeared searching for Flight 19

The Bermuda Triangle extends southeast from Miami, Florida, to San Juan, Puerto Rico, then north to the island country of Bermuda, and then southwest back to Miami (See Figure 5). It covers an area of approximately one million square miles. Over the last 25 years, it is estimated that more than 75 aircraft, along with over 1000 yachts and commercial ships, have disappeared without a trace in the Triangle. I have read many books and stories on this disappearance, along with other disappearances, and some of the reasons vary greatly, from an alien spacecraft, to the ocean looking different, to nothing unusual at all besides the planes getting lost.

My theory when I was younger was all of the ships and planes that disappeared were all the work of aliens. Instead of abducting one person at a time here and there, why not abduct whole ships and airplanes in an area where there was a lot of shipping and airline traffic? It made complete sense to me at the time.

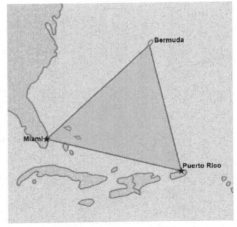

Figure 5 - The Bermuda Triangle

14

The more I read, the more I became interested in ghosts, poltergeists and haunted houses, especially because of some stories I read and movies I had seen. The first story that really got me interested in the supernatural ran in the old *Cleveland Press* newspaper. During the Halloween season, the Press used to print "true" stories on strange and ghostly happenings. One of the stories I read was about moving coffins in a family burial vault on the island of Barbados in the Southern Caribbean. The Chase Family Vault,[11] which is located in the cemetery of the Christ Church Parish Church in Oistins, Barbados, was the scene of unexplained incidents during an eight-year period from 1812 until 1820. Whenever the vault was opened to accept another family member, the previous coffins that were already inside would be found in disarray. It was like some unseen force threw them about inside the vault. This happened five times during the aforementioned time period. It came to the point that the vault would be sealed and sand spread on the floor of the vault to detect any intruder's footprints. Yet each time the vault was opened, it was found that the seals were unbroken and there would be no footprints in the sand, and the coffins would still be in disarray! After the fifth incident, the Chase family could not take it anymore and the vault was abandoned and the coffins buried elsewhere. The Chase vault is still there, but to this day it has remained empty.

Then, a made-for-TV movie came out in 1978 that fascinated me, called *The Ghost of Flight 401*,[12] starring Ernest Borgnine. *The Ghost of Flight 401* is based on a true story stemming from the crash of Eastern Airlines, (Lockheed L-1011 TriStar #310 - See Figure 6) Flight 401[13]. Flight 401 crashed on December 29, 1972 into the Florida Everglades while on approach to Miami International Airport from New York City. In all, 94 passengers, two flight attendants and three crew members, including the pilot Bob Loft, co-pilot Albert Stockstill, and flight engineer Don Repo, all perished in the crash. There were 78 survivors.

After the crash, parts of the damaged plane were salvaged and installed on other Eastern Airline planes and even used by another airline. In those planes where the salvaged parts were used, the ghosts of the pilot Bob Loft and flight

Figure 6 – An Eastern Airlines L-1011 similar to Flight 401

engineer Don Repo started appearing to crew members and passengers. What I thought was amazing about those sightings was the ghosts actually spoke to the witnesses, which included flight attendants, pilots, flight engineers and even one of the vice presidents of Eastern Airlines. One of the ghostly incidents occurred in the galley of an airborne Eastern Airlines flight. A flight attendant who was working in the galley saw the face of Don Repo in the oven's glass. She became frightened and called for two of her colleagues to come down to the galley. One was the flight engineer who was a friend of Repo's. Once he entered the galley, he immediately recognized the face of his deceased friend. All three witnesses then heard Repo say, "Watch out for fire on this airplane." A short time later, the airplane experienced a major engine malfunction, when one of the engines caught fire. Because of this, the last leg of the flight had to be canceled. The galley on this flight happened to be the galley salvaged from Flight 401. Creepy, if you ask me! That scene in the movie affected me the most emotionally. What was interesting about this one incident was the ghost was clearly recognizable, he spoke to the witnesses, he predicted the future and all three witnesses both saw and heard him. The movie sent chills up and down my spine, and in fact, still does.

My interest in ghosts and haunted houses really took off in 1977 when a book came out written by Jay Anson called *The Amityville Horror*.[14] To me, this was the granddaddy of all books based on a real haunted house. This book scared the crap out of me more than any other book I had read up to that point or since. Even the look of the house with the quarter octagon windows that looked like eyes sent a chill up and down my spine (See Figure 7). The book, which is set in Amityville, Long Island, New York, tells the "true" story of

George and Kathy Lutz, who, along with their three children, moved into a large colonial house in December 1975, only to flee 28 days later, claiming they were terrorized by paranormal occurrences and demonic activity. The previous family who lived in the house was murdered by the eldest son, Ronald Defeo Jr.[15] He shot and killed six members of his family while they were sleeping in late 1974. In his trial he told the court how voices in his head told him to kill his family.

Figure 7 - The Amityville House

I could probably write a book just about the Amityville Horror, but that's already been done, so I will just leave it at that.

My father, who passed away in September 2008, and I used to have lengthy discussions—arguments if you will—about the existence of ghosts and UFO's. He never believed in all that stuff, and I was always trying to convince him that they did exist. He was always trying to tell me they didn't, and that it was all a bunch of hogwash.

I wish I could have proven him wrong before he passed. Just like father and son, we both thought we were right. I do have to say though that he became more interested in the paranormal after I started investigating more. He would always ask how the investigation went, and if I captured any evidence. He was amazed at some of the evidence I showed him. Maybe he was starting to come around a little. Too bad he hasn't come back to let me know he's still around, or has he? Maybe now he realizes there is more going on in this universe than we can understand or explain.

So, that is how I became fascinated with the paranormal and the unknown, not by living in a "haunted house" or having numerous paranormal experiences, but by reading books, watching movies and just having an imagination. I really wanted to see a ghost more than anything, just like I wanted to see a UFO, but I believe certain people are more perceptive and receptive with the paranormal than others. I would have probably crapped my pants and screamed my lungs out if I would have seen a ghost, especially if it was standing next to my bed while I was sleeping! You know the old saying, "The dogs with the loudest bark are the ones most afraid." That would have definitely been me!

I continued to watch science fiction and horror movies, and still read books. Other than that, I never really got more involved in the paranormal. That would change in May 1991.

CHAPTER TWO

MY FIRST INVESTIGATION:

THE GREEN GHOST

Before I get into my first investigation, I think it's important to share a little bit of my background. My father, mother, younger sister and I moved to Twinsburg in the spring of 1963 when I was five years old. I grew up in Twinsburg, Ohio, graduating from R.B. Chamberlin High School in June of 1976. After graduation, I immediately enlisted in the United States Air Force and spent my entire tour (1976-1980) stationed at NORAD (North American Air Defense Command) in Colorado Springs, Colorado. I wanted to enter law enforcement to become a police officer in the military, but my father talked me out of it, saying I was too shy to approach people to start a conversation. I guess I was kind of shy during my high school years, so I opted to be trained in Aerospace Control and Warning, which basically meant I watched radar scopes.

I moved back to Twinsburg in the summer of 1980 after my enlistment was up. I decided to follow my heart and not my father's advice, and applied to the City of Twinsburg Police Department as a police officer. I was eventually hired in March 1982 to begin my career in law enforcement. Guess I wasn't so shy after all. This was a dream come true for me because I wanted to be a Twinsburg Police Officer ever since I was in high school. I was a police officer in the town I grew up in, and I knew the town and people really well, which made it easy for me starting out in my new career. However, at that time I really knew nothing about any "haunted" locations in Twinsburg.

In the late 1980's I learned about a strange house from one of the "old-timers" on the department. The house was located in a secluded location off of one of the main roads that went through the City of Twinsburg. I also learned that the house was abandoned by the previous owners and that they left everything behind. My interest in this abandoned house was piqued and I asked my supervisor if he would take me there. He agreed so off we went in our patrol cars so I could see it for myself. We pulled off the main road and drove up an old, abandoned, broken asphalt driveway that was overgrown with bushes and weeds. At one point I didn't think my cruiser would make it up the hill and through all the overgrown brush. At the end of the driveway, there it was, a large two-story, split-level house, which was overgrown with weeds and bushes, hiding it from the roadway. The paint was peeling, and the majority of the windows were broken. Gutters hung in disrepair, and large tree branches bent over gently touching the roof of the house like some large, boney hand. There was even a rusted and abandoned car sitting in the weeds in back of the house. Here was this large house, sitting several hundred feet from one of the busiest main roads in the city, and I never knew it existed, even after being on the police department for several years. We exited our patrol cars and entered through a rotted rear door that we had to forcefully push open because the bottom of the door rested on the warped floor. The inside of the house was pretty much a disaster. The paint on the walls was peeling and there was water damage and rotted wood throughout from years of neglect. The strange thing was it appeared that all of the previous homeowners' belongings were still there. There was still furniture in the house and dishes in the cupboards. There were wall decorations and paintings that still hung on the walls. It's just as if the family woke up one day, and for whatever reason, decided to leave everything they ever knew and owned behind. My supervisor told me the previous family just up and left in the late seventies, and moved out of state. From what I was told, they even left several guns behind, which were taken by the police department for safekeeping. You definitely shouldn't leave those in the house, because I'm pretty sure that local teenagers from the city used the house as a local party place and hangout.

After that initial visit, I would go up there by myself on occasion, and wonder why the family left in such a hurry. Could it be the place was haunted, and they were afraid to live there one more day? Was it another "Amityville Horror House"? Why would they leave everything behind? I couldn't figure it out, and no one I talked with had any other ideas either. I never did find the answers to these questions, but it piqued my curiosity in the paranormal again. Eventually the city tore down the house as it was a safety hazard.

Then something happened in May 1991 that really got me interested in investigating the paranormal—something that would change my life forever.

One of my fellow police officers talked openly about how he believed his house was haunted. He told me there were strange things going on that he could not explain.

The house, which was built around 1940, was a small, 1,000-square-foot, two-bedroom ranch. Besides the two bedrooms, there was a great room, which consisted of the living room, small kitchen and dining room in the front of the house. Situated at the rear of the house was a small den and one bathroom. There was also a basement with a dirt floor and a detached one car garage located behind the house. The house sat at one of the highest elevations in the city. It was said by neighbors that the house was moved to its current location from another location down the road.

Dale* lived there with his wife, his 11-year-old daughter, and 13-year-old son. He stated they were all experiencing strange occurrences at one time or another while living in the house. One evening, while his daughter was taking a shower, she heard a voice calling her name. When she got out of the shower, she asked her dad what he wanted. He said he didn't call her, and no one else in the family called her name either. Other occurrences happened in the kitchen where silverware would be moved about, and a shadowy figure was observed standing near the sink. The lights in the master bedroom would turn on by themselves, and mysterious footsteps would be heard throughout the house. The master bedroom also continuously smelled like iodine, even though the owners repeatedly cleaned the bedroom in an attempt to get rid of the smell. Even their dog refused to enter the master bedroom. Yet the strangest occurrence of all occurred when Dale woke up in the middle of the night to see a figure of a woman surrounded in a sickly green luminescence floating throughout the bedroom. The ghostly figure was only visible from the chest up. According to Dale, he was able to clearly see that she was wearing a button-up dress blouse that appeared to be in style during the 1930s or 40s. Folks in the area claim that a woman was killed in an automobile train accident just down the road from where the house currently sits, and near the area where the house was originally located. I have been unable to confirm that this tragedy actually occurred. However, the story could confirm what Dale and his family were seeing and hearing.

---

* Name Changed

There was another instance when Dale awoke in the middle of the night, and saw the same ghostly figure floating throughout the room. This time, he woke up his wife, and together they watched the figure float throughout the room until it disappeared.

When Dale told me about what was happening in his house, I was fascinated and curious as to what was causing all the ghostly phenomenon. Here was the opportunity I was waiting for. I now knew someone who actually was living in an alleged haunted house! I suggested to Dale that we set up my camcorder in his bedroom to see if we could possibly capture the ghostly female on video. He readily agreed to the idea as he wanted to get to the bottom of things also. At that time, the only camcorder I had was one of those large VHS cameras that you had to rest on your shoulder to film. It was pretty much all they had back then. Back in the early 90s, video cameras were not commonly equipped with night vision capability. I never needed night vision at the time anyways because I pretty much only used the camcorder to record my children's birthdays, holidays, vacations, parties, etc., but it was all we had, and it would have to do. I hoped we would be able to capture a green, glowing, ghostly figure even if it was pitch black. Dale thought it was a great idea and was just as excited as I was to see if we would catch anything. So on the evening of May 31, 1991 at around 10:00 p.m., we set up the camcorder in his bedroom. We set the recording speed on the camcorder to EP (extended play), which gave us about six hours of recording time on a standard VHS tape, allowing us to record all the way to 4:00 a.m. A VHS camcorder offered three speeds: SP, or standard play, allowed about two hours of recording time, LP, or long play, was used for roughly four hours of recording time. I pressed record on the camcorder, and then left the house to go home. I was extremely excited about the possibility of catching

23

something paranormal, and couldn't wait for the next day to see if we captured anything on the video.

The next morning, I woke up bright and early, and called Dale. I asked him if anything happened during the night. He said nothing happened while they were sleeping, but when he reviewed the video, he discovered something that was recorded that he couldn't explain. He didn't know if it was a flaw in the video tape or what it was, but I needed to get over there to look at it. I hurried over to Dale's house as fast as I could, and since we lived pretty close, I was there in about 10 minutes. I was excited to see what we had captured! When I arrived, we connected the camcorder to his television in the den, and played the video. The time on the video showed 1:14 a.m. Except for a couple pinpoints of light that were in the room, the screen was jet black. You couldn't make out any features in the bedroom—not the bed, not the dresser, nothing. A humming sound coming from the window air conditioning unit, was the only noise that we could hear in the video. After watching the video for a couple of seconds, the screen started to distort, roll, and jump around as if there were some sort of electrical interference. The interference even affected the sound, which was going in and out in sync with the distortion. At one point, the whole screen went completely blank for a second, which is hard to imagine as the screen was pitch black. Just then, among all the interference, a green-colored, glowing, pulsating light appeared on the screen. It appeared to be coming from the floor at the foot of the bed, since that is one of the areas we had the camera focused on. It was glowing so brightly, the whole screen was cast in a sickly green color. Wow! It lit up the whole screen! You could even see the outline of the end of the bed as the light came up from the floor. At 1:15 a.m. the light disappeared and the electrical interference stopped. It wasn't the figure of the woman we had hoped for, but this was so cool and it definitely was not a glitch on the

24

video tape. It was a brand-new, unopened tape that I put in the camcorder. We tried to figure out what could cause the glowing light, and even though we were both police officers, and thought logically, we had no clue. There had to be some sort of logical explanation, we both reasoned. I then took the video tape back to my house, excited to show my wife at the time and her mother who was visiting from out of state.

When I arrived home, I put the video tape into my VCR. We all sat down to watch. At 1:14 a.m., the electrical interference started, and the tape started jumping around as it did when Dale and I watched it. Before I knew it, the time on the video was at 1:15 a.m., but where was the green, glowing light? It wasn't there! I was dumbfounded! My wife and mother-in-law thought I was crazy, but I assured them the light was there earlier. Where did it go!? I contacted Dale, and told him what happened. I then went back to Dale's with the video tape. We played the video tape again in his VCR, and there was the light, pulsating and glowing in its eerily ghastly glow! What the hell is going on, I thought? How could it be there one time, not there the next time, and then there again? I was completely baffled by this strange set of occurrences. I think it would have been easier to explain a video of a green, ghostly figure of a woman floating around the bedroom than trying to explain what was going on with the video tape.

Over the next several days, I tried playing the video tape on any VCR I could find, but no matter when and where I played the tape, there was no green, glowing light. There was nothing there except the electrical interference! This was getting frustrating because we know what we saw. At one point I even got smart enough to disconnect my VCR, and bring it to Dale's house where we hooked it up to his television. I logically thought that this had to work. I pressed the play button on the video camera, and waited anxiously. There it was! There was the light exactly where it was supposed to be! This was getting more baffling and frustrating by the minute! It would play on my VCR at his house, but not at my house. No matter what I tried, I could not get the light to show up anywhere else. The ghostly light would only show up while playing in a VCR at Dale's house, and nowhere else. There must be something to his house that would only let us play it there.

Now my dilemma was how to fix it so we could show the light to others without having to go to Dale's house all the time. I decided the only way we could get the light to appear anywhere else was to actually set up my camcorder in Dale's house and record the video while it was playing on Dale's television. Logically, it had to work, but who knows with all the bizarre things that were going on? So, that's what we ended up doing and it actually worked! The only problem though was the new video lost a lot of the quality and clarity by having to record it from the television. The video was no longer jet black, but a grayish hue, but at least we could now show our video of possible paranormal activity to others anywhere we wanted (See Figure 8).

I never even thought about investigating the house further. If we did, no telling what we may have captured. I was just excited I captured something on my first so-called investigation. Maybe if we would have gone further in investigating, we might have found some answers.

I wish I knew more about how to investigate back then, especially how to use audio tape recorders to capture EVPs (Electronic Voice Phenomenon). It was a start, and I knew I would get better at investigating the paranormal.

Dale has since moved from that house. I always thought about contacting the new homeowners to see if they were experiencing anything unusual in the house. I decided against it though, in fear of scaring them or causing them to think I'm sort of a whack job!

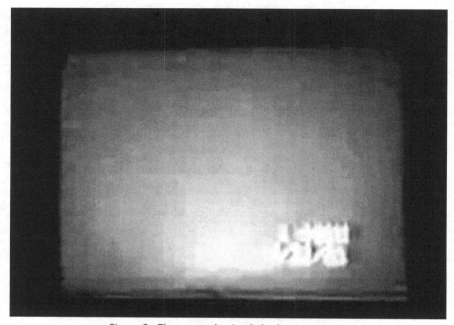

Figure 8 - The green glowing light, bottom center

It's been a long time since that video was first recorded. I still have the original, as well as a taped copy in my possession. Every once in a while I will view the video to try to figure out what it was we captured that night. I still cannot find any reasonable and logical explanation. I guess that's why they call it the paranormal, because surely nothing was normal in this case!

CHAPTER THREE

A HAUNTING IN MISSOURI:

PLAYFUL GHOSTS

In 1994, my sister Shelley and her family moved from Houston, Texas, to a historic home in Moberly, Missouri[16]. Moberly is in Randolph County, located in the north central part of the state, about 40 miles north of Columbia, Missouri. The population in Moberly, according to the 2000 US Census, was 11,945.

The house, which sat on top of a hill overlooking Rothwell Lake Park, was a three-story 3,681-square-foot colonial-style home built in 1924. Looking at the house reminded me of something from an old horror movie or an old silent movie star's home. The house was cream-colored with a stucco finish and brown trim, with a Spanish adobe look. On the first floor was the modern kitchen, dining area, half bathroom, large foyer, large living room, formal dining room, mud room, and Jacuzzi room. The second floor consisted of three bedrooms, a master-suite bedroom with sitting area, and two full bathrooms. The third floor contained another bedroom and a large open area that was originally used as a dance floor for parties back in the 1920s and 1930s. Shelley's husband Jim turned this area into a bar and billiard room for entertaining. There was also a basement and two-car garage situated underneath the house.

I had stayed in their home several times in the past without any paranormal incidents, until one night a few days before Christmas in 1997. I was going through a divorce at the time, and went to visit with my sister and her family for the holidays. It was a trying and depressing time for me as this was going to be my first Christmas away from my three young children who were four, seven, and eight years old at the time. However I don't think my depressed state was the reason I had this paranormal experience. There were sad and depressing moments throughout my life, just like everyone else's, but I never had any paranormal experiences because of them.

The bedroom I stayed in was the guest bedroom, which was located on the second floor (See Figure 9). The second floor also contained the master bedroom and my niece's bedroom, and my nephew's bedroom. This is the same room I always stayed in whenever I would visit. The room was creepy enough during the day with all the ceramic masks and doll faces that decorated the room, but at night, there was a different feel and ambiance in the room that gave it a stranger feel. There was also a balcony with French doors adorned with light, sheer curtains that faced out toward the rear driveway. At night the light from the outside cast eerie shadows in the bedroom from the moon and rear security lights (See Figure 10).

Figure 9 - The Guest Bedroom

I had already spent several uneventful nights sleeping in the guest room prior to this particular night. The night was Tuesday, December 23, and this was going to be my first personal experience ever at 39 years of age.

Figure 10 - The back of the house showing the guest room balcony

Since it was the holiday season, my sister used the spare guestroom to store all of the Christmas presents. There were numerous presents in plastic bags stacked in the corner of the room between the balcony and closet doors (See Figure 11).

I went to bed around midnight, and slept soundly for several hours. Around 3:00 a.m., I woke up and went to use the bathroom, which was becoming a nightly routine as I was getting older. I returned to bed and started drifting off again when all of a sudden very distinct and loud sounds came from the corner of the room where the presents were located! My heart skipped a beat as it scared the living daylights out of me! It was like someone or something was moving the bags and boxes around the room in search of their Christmas present! I immediately sat up, and turned on the light switch, which thankfully was right next the bed. I was extremely relieved and thankful I did not have to cross a dark room to turn on the light! Who knows what I may have bumped into! As soon as the light came on, I was already staring in the corner where the sounds were coming from, hoping to catch a glimpse of whatever was making all that racket. My first thought was it had to be one of their pet cats that somehow managed to sneak into the bedroom with me. There are two doors to the room, and I kept both of them shut, except when I had used the bathroom just a minute or two earlier. But, there was no cat or anything else that I could see. I thought I would have caught a glimpse of a cat scurrying away to some dark hidden recess, but there was nothing! Just the presents exactly how they were when I went to bed that night. I don't know why, but I decided not to get out of bed and search the room. Probably because I was frozen with fear! Instead I just sat there searching with my eyes. The noises were very loud and very real, and I know I was not dreaming as I had just gone back to bed, and had not yet fallen back to sleep. I couldn't figure out what caused those noises. Reluctantly, I turned off the light and lay back down. I lay there motionless, every muscle tensed, ready to spring up if the plastic bags and presents started moving again. I lay there for what felt like hours, but was probably more like 15 minutes before I fell back asleep. If there were any more noises or disturbances throughout the night, I did not hear them.

Figure 11 – The corner of the bedroom where the packages were kept

When I woke up that morning, I searched the room again for one of the cats. If there was a cat in the bedroom it would have still been there since both doors were still closed when I woke, but there still were no cats to be found anywhere in the bedroom. When I saw Shelley that morning, I told her what happened to me during the night. She said it was probably one of the cats. I explained to her that it wasn't one of the cats because there was nothing there when I turned the light on, and there were no cats in the room when I searched it in the morning. She then suggested it could have been a mouse. "Yea, if it was the size of a dog" I answered sarcastically! Both of us then tried to come up with a logical explanation. We now knew it couldn't have been one of the cats, and it definitely wasn't a mouse. We were a hundred percent sure of that. We thought it could have been the heating system. There is a register in the ceiling directly above where the presents were. Hmmm, that is a possibility. We turned up the heat to see if it would make the bags move, but the heat that was blowing out of the vent wasn't even strong enough to move the sheer curtains that were hanging near the balcony doors. That wasn't it then-we were stumped. No matter how hard we tried, we could not come up with a logical explanation. Being a police officer, this really bothered me because I was trained to deal with facts. You know, Joe Friday's saying from the old television show *Dragnet*, "Just the facts, ma'am." All of us older folks would remember that show. The younger ones – probably not. But, here, the facts were not adding up.

I stayed for several days after that night, but nothing ever happened again. In fact, nothing ever happened to me again while visiting and staying there since.

A couple months later I was talking with my Aunt Marge, and the conversation turned to what I experienced with the plastic bags and presents moving in the guest bedroom while staying at Shelley's. My aunt expressed amazement at what I experienced because she stated the same thing happened to her and my uncle while they were staying in that same room the Thanksgiving before. She explained while they were sleeping, something or someone was going through their bags that they had placed in that same corner. My uncle immediately turned on the light and searched the room, but he could find no living thing that could have caused all that commotion.

We never did find the reason behind the commotion in the guest bedroom. However, Shelley confided in me that she, her son and her daughter were experiencing other unexplained and frightening encounters in the house.

One night my nephew, who was in his early teens at the time, was sleeping in his bedroom, which was located just across the second floor foyer from the guest bedroom when he was awakened by his pet dog growling with its eyes focused on something in the corner of the bedroom. When my nephew looked in the corner, he saw a dark, shadowy figure about three feet tall crouching down trying to hide. He flew out of his bed, and ran into his parents' bedroom screaming with his dog following close behind! His parents asked him what was going on, and he excitedly told them there was something in his room. They all went back to his room, and searched, but there was no one there. He ended up sleeping in his parents' bedroom the rest of the night, and the rest of the week!

Another time, Shelley and her son were playing with a Ouija board in the master bedroom, a large suite that consisted of a living room in addition to the bedroom portion. There was a pile of just-washed, folded underclothes sitting on a table in the bedroom. They left the room, and after a minute or so, returned to play with the Ouija board some more. During this session, the board spelled out "L-O-O-K-O-N-F-L-O-O-R." They looked around the room, wondering what the strange request meant. On the floor near the table were the neatly folded clothes, which just a few minutes earlier were sitting on the table! Now they were neatly piled on the floor! Figuring someone was playing a trick on them, they searched the whole house, but could find no one. This really freaked them out, but there had to be a logical explanation. They went back to the Ouija board and started another session. We always thought there had to be logical explanations for the strange things that were occurring, but when dealing with the paranormal, nothing is logical! This time the board spelled out "L-O-O-K-D-R-E-S-S-E-R." When they looked at the dresser, they discovered Shelley's underclothes drawer open with some of the contents hanging from the drawer and the rest scattered on the floor! That was enough! They immediately stopped playing, and got rid of the board! It was probably too late, though. More than likely, they opened a door to the other side, and it probably wasn't a good door either!

Shelley's daughter, who was also in her early teens, also had strange encounters while living in the house. She did not like sleeping in her own bed and would sleep in her parents' bedroom. She said she always heard people on the third floor walking around and laughing, like there was a party going on. She also would see shadows and hear strange noises throughout the day in the house.

One night, she decided to try to sleep in her own bedroom. From her bed, she could look directly into the guest bedroom, which was located across the second floor foyer hall. Her bedroom was right next to her brother's bedroom. This night she was sleeping in her bed with the bedroom door open, when something awakened her. She looked out her bedroom door and into the guest bedroom where she saw a dark figure standing there staring at her! Like her brother before her, she screamed and ran down the hall to her parents' bedroom. Again, they went back and searched her bedroom and the guest bedroom, and just like before, there was no one there. Since that night, she never slept in her bedroom again, instead opting to sleep on the sofa in her parents' bedroom.

One of the last frightening occurrences in the house happened in late 2008 shortly after our father passed away. Shelley, as the only one home, was watching television in the master bedroom when she heard heavy footsteps ascending the wooden, creaky stairs to the third-floor ballroom. When the footsteps got to the top, the door at the top of the stairs opened, then closed shut! Shelley became extremely frightened and nervous because she thought someone had broken into the house. She locked herself in her bedroom and called her husband Jim at work, who immediately rushed home. I don't know why she didn't call the police first, but thankfully he only worked down the street so he was home within several minutes, but I'm sure it felt like an eternity to Shelley. Once he got home, he proceeded to search the house for an intruder, but just like all the other times, no one could be found.

What was causing all of the activity in the house? Could playing with the Ouija board have caused some of the activity? I guess that is very possible. There is, however, a great controversy surrounding the use of Ouija boards. Some people swear they are an evil that can open doors, and invite things you really don't want into your home. Others claim it is nothing more than a child's game. Here is something very interesting to know about Ouija boards. They were never considered evil until the movie *The Exorcist*[17] came out in 1973. In the movie, Regan, the little girl who became possessed, was playing with a Ouija board prior to her becoming possessed. Because of Hollywood, people believed Ouija boards were nothing to be trifled with. Hollywood makes up a lot of things that people take for the truth. Are Ouija boards really any different than trying to communicate with the other side by the use of pendulums, dowsing rods, séances or even an EVP session using audio recorders? It's probably better to be safe than sorry. Why take the chance using one?

Another theory regarding the mysterious activities of my sister's house leads to circumstances surrounding the previous owner. After my sister purchased the house, she and her husband decided to remodel the interior. Since the house was well known throughout the community, they decided to have an open house. They invited the previous owner, but she declined, saying she wanted to remember the house the way it was. Shortly thereafter, she passed away. Did the previous owner return and make her displeasure known about the changes to "her" house? There have been reports that paranormal activity will increase during and after a house is remodeled.

We never did find out what caused the bags and presents to move when my aunt and uncle, and later I, stayed in the guest bedroom. Maybe it was one of my sister's pets who passed on, and they were merely playing and having a good time with the plastic bags. After my sister and her family moved from the house in 2010, the new owner had the house torn down. Maybe he heard about all of the activity occurring in the house or maybe he had some unsettling occurrences of his own and decided it was best not living there! We will probably never know the truth.

CHAPTER 4

SAVANNAH, GEORGIA:

AMERICA'S MOST HAUNTED CITY

In September 2003, my wife and I visited Beaufort, South Carolina to attend her son's graduation from the United States Marine Corps at Parris Island. While we were in South Carolina, and since it was so close, we decided to take a short drive to Savannah, Georgia[18]. Neither of us had ever been there, but we heard it was a beautiful city, and haunted. Ah, extremely haunted! You didn't have to ask us twice! That's what we live for, so we jumped at the opportunity to visit one of the most haunted cities in America.

The City of Savannah was founded in 1733 by General James Oglethorpe, a British general, Member of Parliament, philanthropist and founder of the Colony of Georgia. He was a social reformer who hoped to resettle Britain's poor, especially those in debtor's prisons in the New World.

Savannah, which gets its name from the Savannah River, was the first state capital of Georgia. The name Savannah comes from a group of Shawnee who migrated to the area around Piedmont, in the late 1600's. The Shawnee were called by several variant names such as Shawano, Savano, Savana, and Savannah. It is the oldest city in Georgia, and was also the first pre-planned city in America, built in a grid pattern around four original village squares. At its peak in 1851, there were 24 squares in the city. That number has since diminished to 22 squares in 2010. Nearly every square was the scene of a bloody battle, mass burial site or execution site.

We arrived in Savannah in the late morning, and were taken by the beauty and feel of the city. It is a historical, yet elegant city. It is a modern city that retains its character from its colorful past. In fact, pre-Civil War Savannah was named the most picturesque and serene city in the United States at that time. Everywhere you looked, you could see the architecture, with historic buildings along the streets, nestled near large oak trees draped in Spanish moss. The city was beautiful, and it was a gorgeous day, so we decided to start our visit at one of the most popular areas for visitors and residents to explore—the River Walk. The River Walk is on River Street, just north of Savannah proper, and is situated along the Savannah River. We strolled along an old cobblestone street lined with numerous shops and restaurants. Along River Street there are plenty of places to just sit and people watch, or to just sit and watch the ships travel up and down the river (See Figure 12).

After spending most of the day checking out all the shops, we decided to get a bite to eat and stepped into one of the many restaurants along River Street. Our waiter was a young man in his late twenties who told us he moved to Savannah the year before. The more we chatted with him, the more we found out about Savannah's ghosts. He said before he moved to Savannah he never believed in ghosts, spirits or anything like that. He told us about his own ghostly experiences after he moved into his apartment and relayed

Figure 12 - A cargo ship travelling down the Savannah River

38

how the doors in his apartment would open and close on their own. On numerous occasions when he would return home from work he would discover the water faucet turned on in the bathroom. He told us he didn't have a roommate, and when he asked the apartment manager if he was entering his apartment, the manager said no. This was the first person we met who lived in Savannah, and he was already talking about ghosts. That probably wouldn't happen at a restaurant in Cleveland, Ohio near where I live, but then again, Savannah is supposed to be one of the most haunted cities in America.

After lunch and further exploration of River Street, we decided to venture into the heart of Savannah, and what better way to see the heart of Savannah than a horse drawn carriage tour? So, off we went in search of a horse-drawn carriage. We didn't have to look far, because as we found out, there are numerous carriage tours to choose from throughout the city.

The carriage tour we chose, Carriage Tours of Savannah[19] (See Figure 13), took us past several of the squares in Savannah, including Columbus, Oglethorpe and Wright squares just to name a few. We rode through the historic district and by spectacular architectural homes and buildings. We rode by Colonial Park Cemetery and the birthplace of Juliette Gordon Low, founder of the Girl Scouts of the USA.

I could go on and on about all the sites and things to do while visiting Savannah, and the surrounding area, but that is for another type of book; a travel guide to be precise. So let us talk about what brought us to Savannah….ghosts.

As I mentioned earlier, the city is beautiful during the day. But after the sun goes down it seems to take on a darker, more mysterious

side. Since we were only in Savannah one day, we decided it would be fun to do one of the many Ghost Tours that Savannah has to offer. I know to some of you it may sound corny, but when you're visiting a haunted city for only one day, you really

Figure 13 – Kathy and the Carriage Tours of Savannah

don't have many options when it comes to investigating haunted locations. Remember, we came down here for the Marine Corps graduation, not to do a formal investigation.

In Savannah, there are several ghost tour options to choose from: ghost walking tours, ghost carriage tours, ghost trolley tours, and even a ghost hearse tour where you ride in an open top hearse! That sounds fun, but it was a bit too much for us, so we opted for one of the walking tours. We met our tour guide at dusk in Reynolds Square, which was designed in 1734 and is named for Captain John Reynolds, Governor of Georgia in the 1850s. There is also a bronze statue in the square, which honors John Wesley, the founder of Methodism.

We began our tour walking south on Abercom Street. Along the way, our tour guide told us a little bit of the history of Savannah, and some of the "minor" hauntings that we would pass along the route we were walking. We then walked west on North Broughton Street, where we made our first stop at The Marshall House Hotel[20].

The Marshall House Hotel (See Figure 14) built in 1851 by businesswoman Mary Marshall, is the oldest operating hotel in Savannah. Toward the end of the American Civil War the hotel served as a hospital for wounded soldiers, both Union and Confederate. When a soldier was wounded during battle in an arm or leg, the chances were extremely high that the injured limb would be amputated. This was because the bullets of that era, called Minié balls[21], caused extensive damage to bone and tissue, making it almost impossible to successfully repair back then. The Minié ball was a large conical-shaped bullet made of soft lead that ranged in

Figure 14 - The Marshall House Hotel

sizes of .54, .58 and .69 caliber. When a Minié ball struck the body, it would flatten out and break apart, causing devastating wounds. Due to the medical inadequacies at the time, and the amount of damage done by the Minié ball, the easiest and fastest way to save a wounded soldier's life was amputation of the injured limb.

After each of the many amputations that were hastily done at the Marshall Hotel, the surgeon would just throw the amputated limbs out the window and then start on the next amputation. Our tour guide told us there were so many amputations at the hotel, and the amputated limbs were stacked so high outside of the window, that it was impossible to throw any more out.

The Marshall House Hotel also served as a hospital during two yellow fever epidemics. The 1854 epidemic killed 1,040 people, while the epidemic of 1876 claimed 1,066 victims within the first two weeks alone, eventually claiming an estimated 1,591 victims.

As I stood across the street from the four-story brick structure, I started imagining what it was like back in the 1860s at the time of the American Civil War. Horse-drawn ambulances ceaselessly rushing wounded soldiers to the hospital. The sounds of the wounded and dying, screaming and moaning in agony, while praying for help and the end to their suffering. Besides my interest in the paranormal, I am also interested in the Civil War. I guess you could call me a Civil War buff, and just like with my interest in the paranormal, I read everything I can get my hands on about the war— the battles, the generals, the enlisted men's lives, weaponry, medical services, and so forth. So, as I stood there, I wondered what was going through the wounded soldiers' minds as they waited in pain for their turn to go under the knife. What were they thinking? Were they ever going to see their loved ones again? Did they feel alone? Saddened? Helpless? Desperate? All of the emotion and suffering was a perfect recipe for their spirits to linger.

Our tour guide told us about the spirits that haunted the hotel, saying there were reports of an apparition of a one-armed Confederate soldier searching for his arm. The guide also said there were numerous reports of ghostly children laughing, playing and running up and down the halls. He further told us of one playful spirit of a young girl who would pull the covers back and tickle the feet of men staying in the hotel. I was thinking that something tickling my feet in the middle of the night would have scared me half to death! That's one of the reasons I don't let my foot dangle off the side of the bed when I'm sleeping. I don't want anything grabbing it in the middle of the night! Why would there be the spirits of young children in the Marshall House Hotel? The spirit of a Civil War soldier yes, but children? Maybe they were the victims of the yellow fever epidemics and died in the hotel. Maybe they were the children of previous owners who use to play in the halls. Either way, the Marshall House Hotel is one of the most haunted buildings in all of Savannah. We may have to stay there on our next visit, and I just hope my feet don't get tickled in the middle of the night!

The next stop on our tour was Wright Square (See Figure 15), which is where Chief Tomo-Chi-Chi, the Yamacraw Indian chief who offered peace to the first settlers, was originally buried in 1739. Wright Square was known as the "hanging square" and permanent gallows were built there so that justice could be served swiftly.

Wright Square is also said to be haunted by the ghost of Alice Riley[22].

Alice Riley was an indentured servant to a horrible man named William Wise. Wise treated her so badly that she could not take it anymore, and so with some help, she

Figure 15 - Wright Square

murdered him by drowning him in a bucket of water. In my research of Alice Riley, I discovered that it was either her husband, a boyfriend or another servant who helped her drown William Wise. Your guess is as good as mine. Both Alice and her accomplice fled Savannah, but were eventually caught and brought back to Savannah to face trial. They were both found guilty of murder and sentenced to be hanged. Alice Riley's accomplice was hanged first. It was discovered just prior to her being hanged that Alice was pregnant with William Wise's child. The authorities postponed the hanging, and waited eight months until the child was born before hanging Riley on January 19, 1735. She maintained her innocence to the end, and it is now said that Spanish moss will not grow in the area she was hanged. What a horrible time that must have been for Alice Riley? Just imagine what she thought carrying that child for nine months and then the day after her baby was born, she was to be put to death. I can't imagine what was going through her mind. But I now understand why Wright Square is extremely haunted, especially being known as the hanging square.

During our tour, the guide explained to us why Savannah was one of the most haunted cities in America. He stated in Savannah's early years, it was a busy port, which unfortunately meant it was also one of the main ports in America for slave traders. Many of the slaves died during the long ocean trips from Africa and often the bodies were just thrown overboard. However, there were still many dead bodies within the bowels of the ships when they arrived in port. When a dead body did reach the port, the body would be removed from the ship, and buried on the outskirts of the city. There were thousands of slaves, and others who lost their lives, who were buried in this manner. As the city grew and expanded, the graves would have to be moved. Families who had loved ones, and who could afford it, relocated their bodies to different resting places. But many, especially the slaves, were not so fortunate. They were not re-interred, and instead had buildings and houses built on top of their graves.

We also visited Colonial Park Cemetery[23], a six-acre cemetery established around 1750 right in the heart of Savannah's Historic District. Here, we were told by our tour guide that the expression "saved by the bell" originated at this cemetery. He went on to say during the late 18th and early 19th centuries, people were afraid of being buried alive. So what they came up with was to attach a length of string from the coffin through the ground to a bell. If you awakened and found yourself in a coffin, you could pull on the string to ring the bell, which would alert a watchman who worked in the cemetery for just that reason. You would then be quickly dug up. In other words, you were "saved by the bell." Can you imagine waking up and discovering you were buried alive? That is one way I would not want to go, lying in a cramped, dark, enclosed coffin, with no food or water, knowing that you are going to die, then knowing you would have to stay like this for days or even weeks before you finally succumbed. No thank you! After further research, I am not sure this story is entirely true. Many of the websites stated the phrase came from boxing. If a fighter was in trouble and at risk of losing the fight, and if the bell rang to end the round, he was "saved by the bell"[24]. I have also heard the term "working the graveyard shift" originated from the cemetery watchman.

Our next stop after visiting Colonial Park Cemetery was the Juliette Gordon Low House[25] at the corner of Bull and Oglethorpe streets. The house is a simple, yet elegant two-story "English Regency" townhouse constructed in 1821. Low, the founder of the Girl Scouts of America, was born in the house on October 31st, 1860, to Willie and Nelly Gordon. Born on Halloween and growing up to be the founder of the Girl Scouts of America? Doesn't seem to fit! But the house does have several resident ghosts, two of whom are her parents Willie and Nelly Gordon. Nelly is the most active spirit in the house, often seen staring out a window, playing the piano or sitting at the dining room table. The house is currently a National Historic Landmark and is open to the public for tours.

The last place we visited on our tour ended up making this the most expensive ghost tour we have ever taken! We walked the short distance from the Juliette Gordon Low House, along Oglethorpe Street to 12 W. Oglethorpe (See Figure 16). The imposing two-story brick structure, with its windows boarded up, was the most ominous-looking place we visited on the tour. Even before we heard about what went on, or goes on inside the massive structure, we knew this was one bad place that definitely looked haunted. If I were a ghost, this is where I would want to be!

Our guide told us the stately residence was once the home of a Dr. Brown who arrived from England in the early 1800s to help fight the many yellow fever epidemics in America at that time. Dr. Brown used the back of this home at 12 W. Oglethorpe as his hospital where he treated thousands of patients. Dr. Brown was fighting a losing battle against the yellow fever, and many of his patients died. He starting becoming distraught over all of the death around him, but what took the greatest toll on him was the death of his wife and

Figure 16 - 12 West Oglethorpe

children, who succumbed to the yellow fever in the house. Legend has it that Dr. Brown became so depressed over the loss of his loved ones that he bricked himself up in a room on the second floor, and starved himself to death. What a great story!

While our group stood in front of the house, the tour guide told us if you peer in the front door window and knock three times on the front door, the ghost of Dr. Brown will rush down the stairs toward you screaming all the way. He also warned us that if we took photographs or videos, chances are that our equipment would break. Yeah, right! I seriously doubted that a ghost would come screaming at you, and I certainly didn't buy his story about the equipment breaking either, but he did know how to tell a good story, and he did put our group on edge, which I'm sure was his plan. For all I know, there may have been an accomplice dressed in a ghost costume inside the house just waiting to pounce. The guide asked for volunteers to peer through the glass, yet for some reason, no one wanted to volunteer. What a bunch of chickens! I was anxious to see a ghost, so I was the first to volunteer. I warned everyone in the group though to make room on the walkway leading from the front door, just in case I did see the ghost of Dr. Brown. I didn't want anyone to get hurt as I ran screaming down the walkway! I bravely (only on the outside!) walked up the steps to the front door with my digital camera in hand, while my wife videotaped my every move. I thought that everyone in the group must have thought that I was the bravest man alive. However, inside I was asking myself, what the hell am I doing? I arrived at the front door and slowly pressed my face to the glass, squinting into the dark room and trying to adjust my eyes. I tensed up as I knocked three times. I waited. Nothing. Whew....that was close. I then took several photographs through the glass into the interior of the house (See Figure 17). My wife was the second person to knock on the door. Again, nothing. One by one, each member in the group walked up to the front door and knocked. No Dr. Brown this night and our equipment didn't break either.

Figure 17 - Looking Inside 12 West Oglethorpe

Is the story of the doctor true? Research into the house revealed that the home was built in 1898, almost 100 years after the doctor supposedly arrived in Savannah. I also found out that no doctor ever lived at 12 W. Oglethorpe and it is more likely that the structure is haunted because it was built over graves, just like numerous other buildings in Savannah, but it did make for a good story and a fun experience.

But this is not the end of this story. Within the week, both of our digital camera and the Hi-8 video camera we used stopped working. The video camera's door jammed and the digital camera started taking off-color photographs. The photographs looked tie-dyed. Luckily, the digital camera was under warranty so we took it in to get repaired. After a couple weeks, a customer service representative contacted us in reference to the repair on the camera. He stated the camera is un-repairable, and they had no idea what was wrong with it, so they replaced the camera with a new one. Well, I guess our tour guide was right about the cameras breaking. He did warn us!

We haven't been back to Savannah since, even though it is one of our favorite cities in America. We would highly recommend Savannah to anyone, especially if you are into ghosts and the paranormal. If you do go, make sure you take one of the many ghost tours they have to offer, but beware of 12 W. Oglethorpe. And remember to turn your cameras off.

CHAPTER FIVE

THE BUXTON INN:

GHOSTS FROM THE PAST

When my wife and I first starting investigating haunted locations, we did so as a family with my two young daughters, Allison and Amy, and my younger son, Andrew. One of the first places we actually investigated as a family was the Buxton Inn[26] (See Figure 18) in the quaint village of Granville, Ohio. Granville is about 25 miles east of Columbus and is home to Dennison College, which was founded in 1831. The Village of Granville was established in 1805 by settlers from Granville, Massachusetts and Granby,

Figure 18 - The Buxton Inn main house

Connecticut, and was laid out like a New England town. Granville's main street, West Broadway, is punctuated with sidewalk cafes, shops and restaurants where visitors are seen strolling around or sitting and chatting with friends and family. One would never know by walking around the streets of Granville that the village and surrounding area has a rich history in haunted locations.

Granville and the neighboring city of Newark are home to several haunted locations, including the Granville Inn and Bryn Du Mansion in Granville and the Old Licking County Jail in Newark.

The suggestion to investigate a haunted inn and spend the night was actually my oldest daughter Allison's idea, who was 15 years old at the time. She was doing research on haunted locations in Ohio, and discovered that the Buxton Inn was haunted. She excitedly told us we should go spend the night there and investigate. She even said that she would pay for her room, which she would share with her younger brother and sister. My wife and I decided we had nothing to lose, especially since they were going to pay for their own room. Besides, it sounds like it could be fun. So on a cold Saturday afternoon in January 2005, we packed up and traveled south from the Cleveland area to spend a night in one of the most haunted inns in Ohio – The Buxton Inn. This would be our third time staying at a haunted inn as a family. We had stayed in and investigated the Cashtown Inn[27] near Gettysburg, Pennsylvania in July 2004, and the Rider's Inn[28] in Painesville, Ohio in August 2004.

The Buxton Inn was originally built in 1812 by Orrin Granger, a pioneer from Granville, Massachusetts. The inn was originally known as "The Tavern," and has been in continuous operation since. In its colorful history, the Buxton Inn served as a tavern, post office and stagecoach stop. Past guests of the inn have included President Abraham Lincoln; author of Uncle Tom's Cabin, Harriet Beecher-Stowe; President William McKinley; Henry Ford, Tony-winning actor Hal Holbrook; actress Jennifer Garner and movie star Cameron Diaz.

The Buxton Inn is reputed to be haunted by the ghosts of Orrin Granger, the original owner, Major Horton Buxton, who owned the inn from 1865 to 1902, Ethel "Bonnie" Bounell, the owner from 1934 to 1960, and a phantom cat, possibly named Major Buxton who belonged to Ms. Bounell.

The ghost of Orrin Granger has been seen wandering the inn by several witnesses. They describe him as an elderly gentleman wearing old-fashioned white or blue breeches. The shadowy figure of Major Horton Buxton has been seen throughout the inn also, though he is most often spotted sitting in the dining room. The ghost of Bonnie Bounell has been seen wearing a blue dress in room number nine, the room where she passed away in 1960. Because of the blue dress, she has become known as the "Lady in Blue." The ghostly cat has been seen roaming the halls and jumping up onto beds throughout the inn.

The Buxton Inn complex is made up of several historic houses situated throughout the property, which surround elegant gardens containing beautiful flowers and water fountains. The main house was built in 1812 and has three guest bedrooms, the inn's original guest rooms. The Warner House, built in 1815, has five bedrooms. Founders Hall was built in 1840 and has a total of six bedrooms. The Pearl Street House was constructed in 1880 and has two bedrooms, and the TY FY Mam House, which was constructed in 1900, has three bedrooms. We stayed in the Warner House (See Figure 19), which is a two-story, federal-style brick building consisting of two bedroom suites on the first floor and three bedrooms on the second floor. There is only one common door to the building, which is on the west side of the house, and one private entrance for each suite. My wife Kathy and I reserved the two-bedroom suite on the first floor called the Gold Suite, which is situated in the front of the house. Our three children stayed across the hall in the two-bedroom Raspberry Suite.

As soon as you enter the Warner House through the main door, you are in a short hallway. The door to the left is the Gold Suite, and the door to the right is the Raspberry Suite. Straight ahead are stairs that lead up to the second floor bedrooms. Our children Allison, 15, Amy, 14, and Andrew, 11 were really excited about staying in the "haunted" inn. They have stayed in haunted inns before, but there was something about this place. They even said they would rather go to the Buxton Inn than Cedar Point in Sandusky, Ohio, which is a top-rated theme park known as the Roller Coaster Capital of the World.

Figure 19 - The Warner House

We settled into our rooms, unpacked and then began exploring the grounds of the inn and the Village of Granville. After exploring for a while, we went back to our rooms and started getting ready for dinner. As Kathy was walking across the hall from our bedroom to the kids' bedroom, she saw a bright, gold-colored light floating down the staircase from the second floor (See Figure 20). She couldn't believe what she saw. She blinked her eyes, and in a second it was gone. Wow, she thought! Did I just see that? She excitedly told us what she just saw, but whatever it was, it was gone by the time the rest of us went into the hallway to see for ourselves. It was the middle of winter, and the inn was pretty vacant. In fact, we were the only ones in the Warner House, and the only ones with keys besides the staff. We are very familiar with "orbs" that are captured in photographs, which, in our opinion, are 99% dust, bugs or moisture. This ball of light was seen by the naked eye—a true "orb." How awesome! We hadn't even started to investigate, and already something had happened. In fact, the Warner House is not really known for any major paranormal activity. It is said that most of the activity takes place in the main house. Maybe it would be our lucky night!

We returned to our rooms after having a nice family dinner at the inn's restaurant. I decided it was a good idea to have some snacks on hand during the investigation that evening so the kids and I walked down the street to a drugstore to purchase some. Kathy decided to stay in the Gold Suite to conduct an EVP session (See Figure 21). EVP stands for Electronic Voice Phenomenon, which means by the use of a recording device, either audio or video, voices are captured that were not heard during the

Figure 20 - The Staircase in the Warner House

session. One of the questions Kathy asked during the session was, "I thought I saw you earlier. Was that you?" She asked this question in reference to the ball of light she saw floating down the stairs earlier. Upon reviewing the audio from the session, what sounds like a Class C EVP can be heard. It sounds like a male's voice saying, "Yes it was."

There are three generally accepted classes of EVPs – Class A, B, and C. Class A is the best and clearest, and is heard and understood by all. Class C is the most difficult to hear and understand, and Class B is somewhere in between.

While Kathy was lying in bed doing the EVP session, she had a strong allergic reaction to something. She started sneezing, her eyes started to water and turn red, and she had to use her inhaler. Her asthma is only triggered by her allergy to cats, but there were no cats in the inn and there were definitely no live cats in the Warner House.

Could Kathy have been having an allergic reaction to a ghost cat that may have been in the room, possibly laying on the bed with her? That doesn't seem possible, but read on to the next incident we experienced inside the Warner House.

Figure 21 - Kathy doing an EVP session in the Gold Suite

The kids and I arrived back at the room a little while later, and put everything we purchased into the mini refrigerators that were in the suites. We left the empty plastic bags on the spare bed in the Gold Suite, the same bed Kathy was resting on when she did her EVP session. All of us were in the kids' suite getting ready for the night's investigation. We left both suites doors open since we were the only ones in the building. Amy and I were standing by the hall door when we both heard a lot of commotion coming from the Gold Suite. It sounded like the plastic bags we left on the bed were moving around in our suite. It sounded like something was playing with them! I looked at Amy in amazement, and she looked at me with a stunned look in her eyes. I said, "Did you hear that?" Both of our jaws dropped and our eyes popped wide open! The only thing Amy could say or do was nod her head up and down and mumble, "uh huh." We both stood there frozen, not sure if we wanted to go inside the room to investigate for fear of what we might see playing with the bags. Some paranormal investigators we were! We yelled for everyone else to come here and told them what we heard. By then, the sounds had stopped. All of us then crept into the room expecting to see some bloody horror cat from Hell, with red glowing eyes! But there was nothing there. The bags were on the bed, but there was nothing else in the room, living or otherwise. I searched the room top to bottom just to make sure that no cat got in, but not one live cat could be found. We then decided to see if we could recreate the noise we heard. So Amy and I went back into her room while Kathy stayed in the Gold Suite with the plastic bags. On our command, Kathy started manipulating the bags to try to recreate the sound. Kathy started playing with the bags slowly at first, but it wasn't loud enough. We told her we could barely hear anything, so she started playing with the bags a little more roughly this time, but it still wasn't the same. Finally, she started shaking them and almost tearing the bags apart. That was it! That was what we heard!

Figure 22 – Sleeping "cat" at the Buxton Inn

Whatever it was moved those plastic bags with a lot of force. But wait a minute—isn't the Buxton Inn haunted by the ghost of a cat? That would make sense then. That's why Kathy had the allergic reaction while lying on the bed, the same bed the bags were on. It's like a ghost cat was playing with bags, just the same way a living cat would do. So, it looks like the room we were staying in is haunted by the resident ghost cat. How cool! The night was just beginning and we hadn't even started investigating yet.

After the incident with the bags, we all settled down from the excitement, and started to investigate the rest of the Warner House.

We investigated both suites, the hall and the stairs. However, we did not have access to the three rooms on the second floor. We then proceeded to the main house where we investigated the dining rooms and room number nine. Since the inn was vacant, we were able to get the keys to room nine, Bonnie Bounell's room. As stated earlier in this chapter, room number nine is haunted by the ghost of Bonnie Bounell who passed away in the room in 1960. Unfortunately, we did not get to meet "The Lady in Blue," as she decided not to make her presence known to us. We further investigated our suites during the night, but it seems our personal experiences were over as nothing else paranormal happened.

However, my daughter Allison was able to capture a Class A EVP on a digital audio recorder while she was sitting on the stairs in the Warner House. Allison was sitting on the stairs by herself, talking to no one, to see if anything or anyone would respond. During her session, she stated she did not hear anyone speaking with her at the time. A few weeks later during a review of the audio, you can hear Allison say, "Yep" on the recording. Shortly after Allison says that, you can very clearly hear an unfamiliar woman's voice say, "Can't help." The voice was definitely not Allison's, and it was definitely not Amy or Andrew's. This sounded like an older woman's voice, and was not Kathy's voice either. Allison was the only one in the hallway at the time, and the voice sounded like it was right next to the microphone! What was she trying to tell us? Does it mean she can't help us or we can't help her? It's too bad we will never find out.

That was the first Class A EVP we ever captured, and it was utterly thrilling to us. It still amazes me to this day some of the EVPs that have been captured during investigations.

The next morning we packed up and left the Buxton Inn and headed back home to review all of the audio, video and photographs that were taken. Unfortunately, nothing else paranormal was captured, but we still thought it was a very successful investigation considering we had several personal experiences, and even captured a couple of EVPs—not bad for a family investigation consisting of amateur ghost hunters.

That was the first time we ever stayed at the Buxton Inn, but it would not be the last. Since then, we have stayed numerous times, but nothing compares to the excitement of that first night we spent there.

Even if you are not interested in investigating or the paranormal, it is still a wonderful place to stay and visit. The ambiance takes you back to a simpler time. The restaurant was top-notch with great food, the staff was friendly and attentive, and the village and West Broadway are nostalgic.

If you do stay there, I suggest you also visit the Old Colony Burying Ground Cemetery, which is a short walk from the Buxton Inn. Ground was broken for the first burial in the spring of 1806, and by the mid-19th century, there had been more than 2,000 interments. Veterans of five different wars, including the Revolutionary War are buried in Old Colony.

When you do stay at the Buxton Inn, may I suggest you bring your inhaler – just in case!

For more information on the Buxton Inn please visit their website at www.buxtoninn.com or call them at (740) 587-0001.

Figure 23 – Guest room at the Buxton Inn

Figure 24 – The Tavern at the Buxton Inn

CHAPTER SIX

PARMA, OHIO:

"I COULD NOT LIVE THERE"

The house in Parma[29], Ohio, is one of the most haunted locations, public or private, I have ever investigated. I don't mean we constantly had things happening, or that we actually saw full bodied-apparitions, as we did not. Yet the intense feelings we felt, the personal experiences we had, and the amount of actual evidence captured, by far, made this small, private home a real haunting in the truest sense of the word. Personally, I could not have lived in that house.

Parma, the seventh largest city in Ohio by population, is a suburb southwest of the City of Cleveland. Parma's population at the time of this writing was over 83,000 people.

Tina* and her husband Joe* purchased the small, unassuming, 1,100-square-foot, two-story colonial in September of 2004. Strange things began to happen right after they moved in, a little at first, nothing too frightening. But, as the months went by, the activity increased to the point where the family was truly afraid, and decided they couldn't take it anymore. They wanted something done so they could live in peace. So in October 2007, the owners, who were friends of my wife Kathy, contacted our paranormal team because they did not know where else to turn.

---

* Name Changed

As in all of our investigations, we like to do research on the location and interview the owners and any witnesses. In this case, the only thing we could find out about the house was that it was constructed in 1952. Tina and Joe then related the following occurrences that happened on a regular basis.

There is a Jesus figurine that sits on top of a cabinet in the kitchen. It once belonged to Joe's grandfather who passed away in 2004. Joe has personally witnessed the figurine slowly turn around by itself. If it is sunny outside, the figurine will turn to face the window. If it is rainy, gloomy or overcast, the figurine will turn away from the window.

Several witnesses, including family members and friends, have observed the rocking chair in the living room rocking on its own, even though no one was sitting in the chair.

Heavy footsteps are occasionally heard coming from the second floor. The footsteps sound like someone or something is angrily stomping around.

One of the most active places in the house is the main bathroom on the second floor. Sometimes when the owners are taking a shower, the door to the bathroom will open. The bathroom will then get really cold, and Tina and Joe will have a strong feeling that someone is in the bathroom with them. They will also see shadowy figures in the bathroom.

Another extremely active area is the basement. One time, Joe was walking on the treadmill in the laundry room portion of the basement when someone or something tapped him on the shoulder. The treadmill faces the wall. When Joe turned around, there was no one there. He has also felt something breathing on his neck while he was walking on the treadmill. Joe stated he sees shadowy figures, and always has the feeling that he is being watched while in the basement. Once while he was down there, he heard a male's voice say "Get out!" to him. It should be noted that a lot of the activity in the basement centers around the treadmill. Joe said they purchased the treadmill at a garage sale. Could the treadmill be the root of the activity in the basement? After all, it is possible for ghosts to attach themselves to an object. This can be especially true if they had a strong attachment to a particular object.

One time Tina added her nine-year-old daughter came up to her, and nonchalantly stated, "I think we have a ghost!" Tina asked her why she would think that and her daughter responded that she was in her bedroom when she heard a voice calling "Mommy."

Now we had all the information we needed to conduct our investigation, everything except for a reason why the activity was taking place. Maybe it had something to do with Joe's grandfather or possibly the pre-owned treadmill as mentioned earlier. Some people believe that a spirit or ghost can attach itself to an object. There have been plenty of stories of people buying an item at a garage sale or antique shop, only to find out later that it was haunted or possessed by some spirit or entity. It appeared there was a lot of activity going on in the house and hopefully we could get to the bottom of it and help Tina and Joe.

We had conducted numerous investigations prior to this one, all of them claiming that there was paranormal activity going on. Most of the time, we came away with no personal experiences, and no evidence of any kind, be it video, audio or photographic. It just makes sense. Let's think about that for a moment. Let's say someone lives in a haunted house, and there is activity going on, but not all the time, maybe just a few times a month. The chances that any paranormal team investigating will be able to capture any evidence, especially in just one night, is slim to none. The team would have to be there with equipment running 24 hours a day, seven days a week. And, who knows how long it would take to have a personal experience or to capture any type of evidence. So enroute to this house, I had no reason to think any differently.

Our team this night, consisted of five investigators, including my wife Kathy and myself. We arrived at the house at 7:00 p.m. and were greeted by Tina and Joe at the front door. They invited us in and, after introductions, gave all of us a tour of the house, explaining in further detail the strange occurrences they have experienced. During the tour, almost all of us had very strong feelings in the hallway on the second floor between the master bathroom and their 9-year-old daughter's bedroom. The feelings were also extremely strong inside the daughter's room. One of the investigators described the sensation as a "heavy feeling" on his chest, almost like when he had an accident and his lung was punctured. Another investigator who happened to be the medium in the group felt a feeling of sadness and depression in the same area. What I was feeling on the second floor was so strong and intense, I wanted to run out of the house screaming. I told everyone, "There is no way I could live in this house." What I felt was a very heavy feeling surrounding me, like I was being suffocated. I have had feelings in haunted locations before, but never like this. It was like in the movies. If you watch horror movies, then you know what I'm talking about. A family moves into their new dream home, and a relative comes over, usually an aunt or mother-in-law, to visit the new home for the first time. As soon as they enter the front door, they get a strange look on their face, say, "I need to leave", and then abruptly leave without an explanation. That's what it was like for me at this house in Parma, Ohio.

Once the tour was complete, and we overcame our initial feelings, we went to work setting up all of our equipment. We placed a total of seven stationary video cameras throughout the house: two in the basement to capture any shadows, one in the living room focused on the rocking chair, one in the kitchen facing the Jesus figurine, one in the upstairs hallway, one in the upstairs bathroom and one in the daughter's upstairs bedroom. We also placed an audio recording device in the upstairs hallway. If anything was going to happen during the investigation, we should be able to capture it.

During our initial setup, base EMF (Electro-Magnetic Field)[30] and temperature readings were taken throughout the house. We do this in case there are any fluctuations during the investigation from the initial base readings. Any change from the base readings could possibly indicate the start of something paranormal. Base temperature readings ranged from 71.3 degrees Fahrenheit in the upstairs master bedroom to 78.1 degrees Fahrenheit in the first floor dining room. Base EMF readings appeared to be on the high end in this house compared with other private homes we have investigated. EMF readings ranged from 0.2 mg to 0.7 mg in the basement to 0.3 mg to 7.0 mg in the master bedroom. Normal readings in houses we investigate are around 0.0 mg – 0.3 mg. Readings will be higher near electrical appliances, outlets and water lines, but these are usually easy to determine.

While setting up, we discovered that the medicine cabinet door in the upstairs bathroom opened on its own. During the initial tour of the house, the cabinet door was closed. After the setup, it was found to be open. When questioned, no one admitted opening the door. Hopefully, this was a sign of things to come during the investigation.

All of our equipment was now set up and it was time for the investigation to begin. One of the things we like to do on a private

Figure 25 - Photograph showing shadow in lower left corner

investigation is take the homeowners out to dinner. We like to do this for two reasons. First, it gives us time to just sit and talk with the owners to get to know them a little, and to see how honest and sincere they are, and to let them know how honest and sincere we are. Second, since no one would be in the house, it would lend the opportunity for all of the equipment to record undisturbed. We all left the house at 9:05 p.m. and went to a local pizzeria. We usually go out for pizza during these type of investigations since just about everyone loves pizza! We returned to the home at 10:39 p.m. after a great meal and conversation to begin the actual investigation.

Then the fun began! Almost everyone in the group had a personal experience. Most of the time, you're lucky if only one investigator has an experience during an investigation, but this one was very different.

My wife Kathy, homeowner Joe and I were investigating the basement where the shadows were reported. I started taking photographs with my digital camera when I noticed a dark shadow beginning to form in the lower left portion of the photograph (See Figure 25). That's what's nice about digital cameras, you can view the photograph immediately after you take it. When I first saw the photograph my first thought, as always, was there must be a logical explanation. I tried recreating the photograph by putting my finger over the flash, and then the lens, but could not even come close to recreating the shadow. I could not explain the shadow, and it was not in any previous photographs nor in the photographs taken immediately afterward.

A short time later Kathy was sitting on the treadmill (See Figure 26) in the basement doing an EVP session when she asked the question, "Can you cause something to fall over?" Immediately after she asked the question, something fell over in the back of the basement. All three of us in the basement heard it. It scared the crap out of Kathy! She couldn't get out of that room fast enough! At first I thought it must have been one of the other investigators walking on the floor above us. I always try to think of the most logical reason first, before even thinking it could be paranormal, but both Kathy and Joe replied that it came from the back of the basement, which I had to agree with. I walked into the area of the basement where the noise came from, but was unable to locate the cause. The whole incident was captured on two video cameras—one stationary camera set up in the back of the basement and a handheld one I was video recording with. There are basically two types of hauntings—residual and intelligent. A residual haunting is one in which there is no interaction between the living and dead. It is like a tape recording that keeps playing some past significant event over and over. An intelligent haunting on the

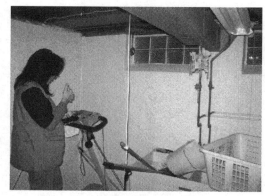

Figure 26 - Kathy near the treadmill in the basement

other hand is one in which ghosts or spirits will interact with you, such as what just happened when Kathy asked if it could cause something to fall over. It looks like we were dealing with a possible intelligent haunting.

Another incident that occurred during the investigation happened when two investigators were investigating the daughter's bedroom upstairs. A stationary video camera set up in the daughter's bedroom recorded the whole incident.

There was nothing unusual about the bedroom, besides being a little cluttered. It was your typical nine-year-old-girl's bedroom with a couple of bookcases filled with books, dolls and stuffed animals. There was a large six-drawer dresser and mirror that had young girls' cosmetics scattered about. The twin-sized bed was covered with a pink, princess and fairytale castle bedspread. There were also several posters on the wall typical to a nine-year-old girl. One thing we did notice were the two crucifixes hanging on the wall above the door frame.

The two investigators were sitting on the floor in the darkened room doing an EVP session. One investigator Jake was sitting near the foot of the bed and the other investigator was seated in front of him. During their session, they heard something fall or move in the corner of the room near the bookcase right behind Jake. Jake looked over his shoulder, but could not see anything because of the darkness in the room. The other investigator asked, "Can you do that again? Can you move something else?" Several seconds later, Jake got poked/pushed in the left shoulder. He lurched forward a bit, let out a little "whoa," and said, "It just hit me on that shoulder." At about this same time, another investigator was "grabbed" on the arm by something unseen while investigating another upstairs bedroom. Both Jake and the other investigator got up and went to the corner of the room where they heard the noise to try to figure out what caused it. Unfortunately, they were unable to find the cause of the noise they heard. However, during the review of this particular incident, something extraordinary was captured on the stationary video recorder that was set up in the bedroom. Both investigators were standing in the corner trying to figure out what fell when an elderly male can be heard on the video asking them, "How's it going?" in a loud clear voice. Both of them did not hear the voice at the time, for if they did, they would have surely responded immediately. But, they just kept talking amongst themselves. It was almost like there was someone else in the room with them who just wanted to be friendly and was curious as to what they were doing. My first thought was that it had to be Jake or the other investigator. There goes the logic in me again! But after listening and analyzing the video clip a hundred times, I knew it couldn't be them. Because this strange voice talked over theirs and it definitely did not sound like either one of them. What an awesome Class A EVP!

Most EVPs we have captured sound whispery, far off and monotone. This one captured on the video camera was completely different. It was clear and there seemed to be feeling and an awareness in the voice. The EVP was so clear and understandable that we thought the voice could be recognized by Tina, Joe or other family members.

The EVP was also captured on a digital audio recorder that Jake was holding in his hand, but this one sounded almost metallic and distant, like it was in another dimension. Very strange.

Kathy and I eventually went back to the house and did a reveal for Tina and Joe. We played the video tape of "How's it going" for both of them to hear. After Tina heard the voice, she said her deceased grandfather used to always say that phrase, but she wasn't 100% sure if that was his voice.

At the reveal we decided to try and see if we could recreate the EVP. We placed the same video camera in the daughter's bedroom. I then stood outside under the window, and started saying the phrase, "How's it going?" Kathy, who was in the bedroom at the time, said she could barely even hear me. When we reviewed the recording, you couldn't hear me at all.

It was decided that Tina would take the recording to her mother and uncle to see if they could identify the voice. After several days, Tina contacted us and said both her mother and uncle positively identified the elderly male voice as their deceased father—Tina's grandfather! There was no doubt in their minds at all!

As with a lot of our investigations with this particular paranormal team, a séance was conducted at the end of the investigation. The séance was held in the second floor hallway. Nothing out of the ordinary happened during the séance, but we did however tell the ghost(s) or spirit(s) that were haunting the house that they needed to stop immediately because they were frightening the family.

Since then, Tina and Joe never had another problem with ghostly happenings in their home, except for one incident where the door knob in the kitchen started to rattle. Tina, who was in the kitchen at the time, yelled and told them to knock it off! Tina, Joe and their family have lived in the house peacefully ever since, and still do to this day.

Who or what was making their lives unbearable? Most likely it was Tina's grandfather who didn't realize he was frightening them. He just wanted to look over and protect his grandchildren. How sad it is to think of someone who loved his family so much that he never wanted to leave. I am sure he is still there watching over them. He just does it quietly now.

CHAPTER SEVEN

THE OHIO STATE REFORMATORY:

THEY'RE HERE FOREVER

When you first drive down Reformatory Road and see the massive castle-looking structure looming to your right, you don't realize it, but the prison already has its hold on you. That's how I felt the first time I saw that awe-inspiring stone structure. I knew it had me in its grasp and would never let go. That was back in August 2004 and it still has its power to hold me tight in its grip to this day.

The Ohio State Reformatory[31] (OSR), also known as the Mansfield Reformatory, was designed by Cleveland architect Levi Schofield. He drew his inspiration for his design from the large castles found in Europe. In fact, the early inmates used to call the prison "The Castle."

The Ohio State Reformatory was constructed in two phases. Construction of the first phase, which included the main administration building and the west cell block, began in 1886. Due to funding problems, it took 10 years to complete. The west cell block consists of 350 cells all constructed of stone.

The first 150 young inmates arrived by train from Columbus on September 15, 1896. They were immediately put to work constructing the 25-foot-high wall that would eventually encompass the entire 15-acre prison complex.

The east cell block was completed in 1908 and consisted of 600 cells housing some 1,200 inmates. The east cell block is currently listed in the Guinness Book of World Records as the largest free-standing cell block in the world.

The prison was built to house roughly 1,900 inmates, but overcrowding conditions pushed that number to well over 3,000 inmates at times.

The prison eventually closed its doors in 1990 because of a lawsuit that was brought on by inmates at the time, claiming brutalizing and inhumane conditions. The last inmates to leave the prison did so on December 31, 1990.

Contrary to popular belief, there were no executions at OSR. The prison still saw its share of deaths though, including several murders.

One such murder occurred in 1932 when 48-year-old prison guard Frank Hanger was bludgeoned to death with a crowbar during several inmates escape attempt from solitary. It is said his ghost still roams solitary to this day.

Another well-known and tragic death occurred in November 1950. Helen Glattke, the wife of Art Glattke who was the warden at the time, was reaching into a jewelry box in her second floor bedroom closet located at the prison, when her husband's service revolver fell onto the floor. The weapon discharged, striking her in the chest. She died three days later from complications, including pneumonia, in a Mansfield hospital. At the time of Helen Glattke's death, wardens and their families resided inside the administration portion of the prison.

Behind the prison, there is a small cemetery where over 200 inmates, who are free at last, are laid to rest. These inmates are now lost to the passing of time, as there are no names on the headstones, just their inmate identification number. They are lost souls due to the fact that family members would not or could not claim the body. Could these lost souls still be trapped behind the massive stone structure that was once their unwanted home for many years? Obviously when dealing with the paranormal, anything is possible. How else can you explain all the strange things that have occurred to visitors, workers and volunteers alike over the years?

After the prison closed, it was scheduled to be demolished by the state to make room for a new prison. In 1995, a group of Mansfield residents formed the Mansfield Reformatory Preservation Society (MRPS) to save the prison. They were successful and eventually purchased the prison from the state of Ohio for $1.00. However, all of the support buildings, as well as the wall surrounding the prison, had already been torn down. The ultimate goal of the MRPS is to restore the prison to its former glory.

Today the prison is a museum (See Figure 27) that offers guided and self-guided tours, ghost hunts and walks, and rental of the facility. The prison has been rented for weddings, proms, corporate events, parties and celebrity events. The prison was also used during the filming of the 1994 movie, *The Shawshank Redemption*, starring Tim Robbins and Morgan Freeman.

The prison also hosts the Haunted Prison Experience during the Halloween season. During the Haunted Prison Experience, the prison is turned into a haunted house where guests have to make their way through the dark. On this trek, they have to walk through horror and ghostly scenes and be on the lookout for all the jumps and scares they will encounter along the way. The majority of the money collected during these events is put back into the prison for restoration.

Figure 27 – Ohio State Reformatory showing main administration

My first visit to the Ohio State Reformatory was in August of 2004. My wife and I, along with two of her friends Maryann and Linda, registered for one of the public ghost hunts that the reformatory conducts throughout the year. There are three types of paranormal ghost hunts the reformatory offers. The first one is not actually a ghost hunt, but a ghost walk. A ghost walk is a two-hour guided walking tour through the prison from 8:00 p.m. until around 10:00 p.m. All of the lights are turned off in the prison. Usually there are anywhere from 20 to 40 people in a group. The tour guide takes everyone on a tour through the darkened prison and visits some of the more haunted locations within. The guides tell some of the ghost stories surrounding the prison, and will let you explore certain areas for a short time. However, this tour is not conducive to conducting an investigation though, because of the number of people in one area, and the time constraints. The minimum age for this tour is 13 years of age.

In addition to the ghost walk, there are two ghost hunts the reformatory offers—a public ghost hunt and a private ghost hunt. A public ghost hunt occurs on most Saturdays throughout the warmer months. During a public ghost hunt, there are around 100 people who participate. The hours are from 8:00 p.m. until 5:00 a.m. and visitors are permitted to explore and investigate practically the whole prison including the basements, and attic. A private ghost hunt is similar, except a group usually schedules it during the other days of the week. There could be anywhere from 10 to 30 investigators who have the run of the prison by themselves for up to nine hours. We opted to do the public ghost hunt for our first time.

We were extremely excited about this ghost hunt, and couldn't wait for the day, or should I say the night, to finally arrive. This would be the first time we did anything like this. I was totally stoked the morning of the investigation, and couldn't wait to get there. When we first pulled down the driveway toward the prison, I was awestruck. The first thing I thought, was, "we're going to be spending the night in there!" This was so cool. I really didn't know much about the prison at the time, but I knew it was large and we were staying the night. That's all I needed to know.

We parked our car, got out and walked to where we checked in. The check-in was located in a small building in the central courtyard directly in front of the administration building. After checking in, we walked around the front of the prison, taking photographs until it was time for the ghost hunt to begin. I must have taken a hundred photographs of the front of the prison from every angle I could think of!

Besides us, there were about 100 other "amateur ghost hunters" that night. Just about everyone had their ghost hunting gear with them, which included flashlights, cameras, EMF devices, video cameras and dowsing rods. I swear some of the flashlights were as big as spotlights! I brought a Sony Hi-8 camcorder with night vision, along with a Canon 35mm film camera. Oh, I also brought my "small" flashlight. I didn't want to blind anyone. Everyone was ready to go, including me. The tour guides split us up into three groups of about 35 people. We were escorted through the main entrance in the center of the building to begin our tour. The guides took us on a tour of the prison to show investigators where all the "hotspots" were located prior to setting us loose. I couldn't believe it. I was finally inside. Even though there were others there, I didn't mind. This was such a cool place!

The guide took us all throughout the building telling us a little about the history of the prison, but mostly about the paranormal activity that has been reported by visitors and volunteers alike. We proceeded to the second floor of the administration building, and were walking down the central hallway that connects the west administration wing to the east wing, when we started to smell a flowery rose scent. The majority of the group smelled it, but we could not determine where it was coming from. It has been reported on occasion that Helen Glattke's perfume could be smelled wafting through the air, especially where she was accidently shot on the second floor. Could that be what we were smelling? After the excitement and talk quieted down, the smell dissipated until it disappeared completely. One thing you do not want to do during an investigation is wear perfume or cologne. However, that was not the case with this scent. We only smelled it for a minute or so, and it was only in that one area. I whispered to my wife that this was going to be an awesome night. We continued with the tour without any more paranormal experiences. After about an hour and a half, we returned to the central meeting location where we checked in. The guides gave us last-minute instructions, and then released us to roam and investigate the building on our own. We were allowed to go just about anywhere we wanted, which was about 90% of the building. And, it was in complete darkness. There were a couple of areas blocked off for safety reasons, but we didn't mind; we had too many areas to investigate as it was.

After last-minute preparations, we headed back to the second floor where we smelled the roses, hoping the smell would return. We walked around the area for a while, filming and taking photographs, but the rose smell did not return. We explored and investigated the administration building for about an hour with no results. We then decided to investigate the cell blocks, making our way down to the ground floor, and after a while, eventually found our way into the cell block. It is difficult finding your way around, and very easy to get lost. We walked along the ground floor of west cell block, looking into cells as we made our way down to the west wing where the west showers and the Jesus room were located. When we got near the end of the west cell block, our friend Maryann decided to stick her head into one of the cells to check it out. When she did, she let out a loud scream that made all of us jump! After she calmed down, she told us when she stuck her head inside the cell door, it felt as if her whole face went through a large spider web. She stated it almost felt like someone's hand pushed her face out of the cell. I have heard that when you are touched by a spirit or ghost the sensation is like that of a spidery cobweb. We checked the cell opening with our flashlights, looking for any signs of spider webs.

We found none. We then proceeded up to the third floor on the west wing, which is known as the Quartermasters room. When we arrived, we discovered other investigators in the room taking photographs and attempting to communicate with the spirits, asking them to give some kind of sign that they were there. We walked around, talking among ourselves and taking photographs, when Kathy tripped and almost fell. She said something tripped her, and she didn't do it herself. She stated it felt like someone or something placed a string or wire about ankle high across the floor. We looked around the floor, but could not find anything that would have caused her to trip. The things we had happen so far were more than we expected, but the night was just beginning, and far from over.

We continued exploring other parts of the prison, including the Jesus Room, solitary, east cell block, east showers, basement and more of the administration portion of the prison. We were investigating the third floor in west administration when Kathy entered a bathroom located on the northwest side of the hall (See Figure 28). Right after she entered, she quickly exited, and said, "I don't like it in there. I think there's something there." Maryann, Linda and I immediately went inside the bathroom, with Kathy reluctantly following behind us. Once we were all inside, we closed the door to the main hall. We sat in total darkness and silence

Figure 28 – Entrance to the bathroom

wondering why Kathy didn't like it in here. We asked her, but she couldn't explain it. It was so dark in the bathroom, you could not even see your hand in front of your face. There were no other investigators in the area we were in at that time, which made it so

76

Figure 29 – The bathroom, showing the ceiling where we witnessed the "light show"

extremely quiet, you could hear a pin drop. We sat there for what seemed like an hour, but was probably only several minutes, before we saw it. Time always seems longer in the darkness! Directly above us on the ceiling (See Figure 29), which was about eight feet high, was a psychedelic, swirling mass of brilliant colors. I called out to everyone, "Do you see what I see?" They all answered yes. All of us were watching the same swirling light show on the ceiling, and we sat there mesmerized watching the lights dance around the ceiling. After watching for several seconds, the lights slowly faded away immersing the room into total darkness again. We immediately turned our flashlights on and searched the room, but could not locate anything that could have caused the lights. We then opened the door and went into the hall to look for someone who may have shone a flashlight in, but we could not find anyone. We then tried recreating the lights by shining flashlights under the closed door, but to no avail. There were no windows in the room, as they were all boarded up, so it couldn't have come from outside. No matter what we tried, we could not recreate those lights. It wasn't our imagination because we all saw the same thing.

We explored, and investigated the prison for the remainder of the night, but we had no more personal experiences. By 2:00 a.m. the majority of the people had already left. It started to get eerily quiet and seemed even darker than it was when we first started. We started getting tired, and by 4:00 a.m., we decided it was time for us to leave also. We still had an hour-and-a-half drive ahead of us. We packed up what little equipment we had, and left the building. As we drove through the gate and up Reformatory Road, we looked back at the prison, silhouetted against the early morning sky. It was beckoning us to return. Don't worry, we will definitely be back.

Since that first investigation, and prior to the printing of this book, I have returned for nine other investigations. Seven of those investigations have been private ghost hunts, and there is no doubt we will be back again in the future.

In September 2007 my wife and I returned to the prison again for a public ghost hunt. This time, it was just Kathy and I, as we did not bring any of our friends. It was later in the night, early morning, when we were walking down the staircase from the second floor to the first floor in the west administration. As we were walking down the stairs, we heard someone sigh right between us. We had our video camera rolling at the time. I asked Kathy if that was her. She replied, "No, I thought it was you." There was no one else in the west administration that we could see or hear. It sounded as if someone was depressed or sad, and let out a big breath of a sigh.

In November 2008, we booked our first private ghost hunt. We invited 30 of our friends and acquaintances to spend the night with us investigating the prison. Two of the people who joined us that night were my step-son Dale and his wife Tina. It was freezing in the prison this time,

Figure 30 – The west cell block tier where we smelled the foul odor

and we were all bundled up with our best winter clothing! Later, during the investigation at 2:21 a.m., we were walking along one of the tiers in the west cell block (See Figure 30). Dale was leading the way with the video camera. About half way across the tier, Dale stopped and said, "That smell's back. Do you smell that?" We all smelled a noxious odor that smelled like rotten eggs or sulfur. It was so strong, it would almost make you gag. We smelled the same odor earlier in the investigation in another area of the west cell block. As quickly as the odor came, it was gone. We thought it was very strange, especially smelling it twice, but didn't think much more of it until I reviewed the video footage of the incident. In the video you can see a foggy cloud that comes from behind us. It then goes through us, and then off to the right over the railing. The rotten egg smell had to be coming from the fog, but what could have caused it, both the fog and the smell? I know rotten or sulfuric odors are associated with negative entities and/or inhuman spirits. Anyone would surely know that a prison would hold a lot of negative energy, considering all of the violent inmates and the violent crimes they committed, both inside, and outside of the prison walls. Could this have been one of those inmates who holds a negative imprint inside the prison? Or could it have been a prisoner who just stunk, because the prisoners were only allowed to shower once a week? Just imagine what it would have smelled like back then. Three-thousand inmates all stinking from the lack of daily showers! As I've said before, anything is possible, especially when you're dealing with paranormal.

During our other private ghost hunts, we have captured numerous EVPs and had several other personal experiences. Some of those EVPs were in result to questions, which is indicative of an intelligent haunting. Here are two examples. For both of these EVPs, we reserved the prison for a private ghost hunt. During one investigation toward the end of the night, one of the investigators asked another investigator, "What happened to the rest of our group?" An EVP responded, "They already left." That group of four was the only ones left in the building, as the rest of us already left for the night. They did not hear it at the time, and it was only discovered during a review of the audio. The other EVP was captured in the library in the wing of the east cell block. An investigator was standing at the counter in the library when she asked the question, "What is this?" The question was in regards to an old phone book sitting on the counter. Another investigator replied, "It looks like an old phone book." However during a review of the audio, another voice was discovered that they did not hear at the time. After the question of, "What is this?" an EVP replied, "Library." It is amazing some of the EVPs that we have captured there.

In January 2013 I decided to do something I have wanted to do ever since seeing the reformatory that first time. I wanted to volunteer my time there. It would be easier now since I was retired from the police department in 2011. I talked my wife into becoming a volunteer there also. We attended the new volunteer meeting in March of that same year. That first year we mostly did "pushing" on the ghost walks the prison offered every once in a while. A "pusher's" job was to keep the group together, making sure no one wandered off. The following year, we became more involved by working some of the events that were held there, including a Mystery Dinner Theater. We continued pushing for ghost walks, and that is where we had, or should I say my wife, had another paranormal encounter. It happened toward the end of one of the ghost walks. The group was in the west administration wing on the first floor. The first floor was originally the main administration offices where the warden's and assistant warden's offices were located. In fact, I always considered the west administration wing to be one of the most haunted locations in the entire prison. Becky, our tour guide, was standing on the staircase leading up to the second floor, telling the group about the paranormal events that have occurred in the west administration area. I was standing behind her on the landing at the top of the staircase. My wife Kathy was standing on the next set of steps up from the landing where I was standing. She was looking down the stairs toward me with her back toward the second floor. Behind her was a set of windows which let light from the outside security lights shine on the staircase wall she was facing. In fact she was able to see her shadow on the wall she was facing. While she was standing there, she saw the shadow of a person walking left to right on the wall in front of her. She immediately turned around to see who was there, but there was no one. She called out for me, and told me what happened. We then searched the second floor, but could not locate anyone or anything that could have caused the moving shadow.

I am still waiting to see my first apparition at the prison. I will even settle for a shadow person. Several volunteers have seen full-bodied apparitions there, and I believe as long as I keep volunteering and investigating the prison that my time will come. I just need to have patience and give it more time. And, who knows what strange things I'll see at the Ohio State Reformatory in the future.

For more information on the historic Ohio State Reformatory, please visit their website at www.mrps.org or call them at (419) 522-2644.

CHAPTER EIGHT

MADISON SEMINARY:

A CENTURY AND A HALF OF HISTORY

Madison Seminary[32], also known as The Ohio Cottage, is a large, unimposing brick structure located in the tiny village of Madison, Ohio. If you drove down Middle Ridge Road, chances are you would probably drive right past it without even giving the building a second thought.

So far, I have investigated Madison Seminary six times, and by far, this is the most haunted location I have ever investigated. This is the location where we have captured more evidence than in any other place that we, as a paranormal team, have ever investigated. I have met several other paranormal teams throughout Ohio and Pennsylvania, and most of them agree that Madison Seminary is their favorite, and most haunted, place they have investigated.

Madison Seminary, as it was originally known and affectionately called today, has a long and colorful past beginning in 1847 when a small frame building was constructed on the current site. Madison Seminary was built to provide education to the residents of Lake County and the surrounding counties. Unfortunately, there are very few written records that have survived this time period.

In 1859, a more permanent brick structure was built to the east side of the original wooden building (See Figure 31). The original wooden building was then converted into a boarding hall. During its heyday, which lasted until 1891, Madison Seminary had 150 students enrolled.

Figure 31 - Madison Seminary

In late 1891, the building was purchased by the Ohio Woman's Relief Corps[33] (WRC), a woman's group of the Grand Army of the Republic, or GAR. The GAR was a fraternal organization founded in April 1866 on the principles of "Fraternity, Charity and Loyalty." The GAR was composed of Union veterans from the various military branches who served during the American Civil War. It was dissolved in 1956 when its last member, Albert Woolson (1847-1956) of Duluth, Minnesota, died.

After the Woman's Relief Corps purchased the building, they changed the name from Madison Seminary to the Madison Home. The WRC purchased the home to render assistance to Army nurses and soldiers, along with their mothers, wives and sisters who had been uprooted from the spoils of the Civil War.

The WRC then constructed the current large brick structure to the west of the older brick building on the site of the original wooden structure (See Figure 32). Carved on the archway over the front door is Ohio Cottage.

Figure 32 - The Ohio Cottage

In 1904, the WRC could no longer afford to maintain the building, so they decided to donate the building to the State of Ohio. The complex at the time was known as the "Home of the Ohio Soldiers, Sailors, Marines, Their Wives, Mothers, Widows, and Army Nurses." That's a mouthful! I'm sure glad they decided to shorten the name.

The WRC Madison Home ran from 1904 until June 1962 when the facility officially ceased operations. The building was then taken over by the Ohio Department of Mental Hygiene and Corrections. This was very disheartening to the widows still living in the building because they were to be returned to relatives or transferred to private nursing homes. This was especially hard on the widows who had no relatives to take care of them in the last years of their lives.

At this time, the name was changed again to Opportunity Village, and it was during this time that an annex building was constructed between the two brick buildings (See Figure 33). It was also during this time that female inmates from the Ohio Women's Reformatory in Marysville were housed here, working as staff, learning nursing skills and other occupations, so they would be prepared when they were released back into society.

Figure 33 - The Annex Building

Apple Creek State Hospital, located outside Wooster, Ohio, also sent mentally handicapped woman to Opportunity Village in the hopes that they could be rehabilitated to live productive lives in society.

For several months in 1964, Opportunity Village also housed aged, senile women from Cleveland State Hospital.

In 1975, Lake County Commissioners purchased the building from the State of Ohio and Opportunity Village closed its doors forever. Since then, the buildings have also been used as township offices.

In 1998, the property was purchased from the county for $28,500 and is currently used as offices and storage, as well as for promoting ghost hunts on weekends.

Madison Seminary, as it is currently called, is listed on the National Historic Register.

As you can see, Madison Seminary had a varied, and very emotional history, housing everything from a school to a halfway house to a nursing home. So you would have to think there would definitely be a lot of energy and imprints in the buildings, which there are!

The original brick building includes two floors, an attic and a basement. There are a couple of offices on the first floor and several rooms on the second floor that look like they used to be classrooms or bedrooms. The steps to the attic are located inside a closet on the second floor. The attic was unfinished and was only used as storage. The basement was also used as storage except for one room we called the "Doll Room" that was kept pretty empty.

The Ohio Cottage building is shaped like a "U" with three floors and a basement. Some of the basement here is used for storage and an office and part of this basement is also used as the central lounge for the many ghost hunters who pay a nominal fee to investigate. The rest of the floors all have rooms about the size of bedrooms or classrooms off the halls, except for the west wing on the third floor. This area appears to be some sort of open hall that may have been used for dances, parties, etc.

The annex that connects the two buildings is used as an office for the plant nursery that sits behind the buildings.

Madison Seminary was featured on one episode of SyFy's television series *Haunted Collector*[34], starring John Zaffis, the nephew of famed paranormal investigators Ed and Lorraine Warren. The series featured a team of paranormal investigators led by demonologist John Zaffis. The team would investigate alleged haunted locations with the hopes of identifying and removing any on-site artifacts or trigger objects that may be the source of the alleged paranormal or poltergeist activity.

Madison Seminary was also featured in a 2011 low-budget movie called *7 Nights of Darkness*.[35] The plot surrounds six reality television show contestants who have to spend seven nights in an abandoned and haunted asylum. The prize for staying all seven nights is a share of $1 million dollars, which was to be split among any contestants who are able to last the whole week. I will not give you the ending just in case you decide to watch the movie.

The first time I had the opportunity to investigate Madison Seminary was in August 2011. There were four of us that first time, and we had some crazy things happen that night!

Even though at the time I didn't know too much about the history or any paranormal activity at Madison Seminary, I was still excited. I would always get excited about new investigations and I still do!

The four of us split up into teams to investigate different areas of the buildings. Jake and Lisa made up one team, and my wife Kathy and I made up the other team. Kathy and I spent the first part of the investigation in the older building, while Jake and Lisa investigated the newer Ohio Cottage. After investigating for a while, we switched buildings.

Nothing really happened during the first several hours, but all of us thought Madison Seminary had the potential to be really haunted just by the looks and feel alone.

Around 1:30 a.m. we all decided to investigate the east wing on the third floor of the Ohio Cottage together. We discovered a posted note on one of the walls that called this area, "The Crazy Nurse Ward." Hmmm, if something was going to happen, this was the area. Why else would someone put that note up?

Once we got up to the third floor, we elected to split up and sit in separate rooms, figuring the chances would be greater for at least one of us to experience something paranormal. It was at this time around 1:46 a.m. when the voice of a male yelling was captured on our video and audio recorders. None of us heard the yell at the time it occurred, but instead discovered it when we were reviewing our video and audio. It sounded like someone was trying to get our attention by yelling "HEY!" Too bad we didn't hear it at the time.

Things really started to happen after that. It was now 1:51 a.m. and we were all in our separate rooms, except Jake, who was sitting on the floor in the hallway. A stationary video camera was set up looking down the east wing from the junction of the main hall and east wing and just outside a door to another small room. Jake was just visible in the camera's viewfinder. All of a sudden, Jake yelled "wooooo wooooo!" and sprang to his feet as fast as he could! He then started backing up down the east wing hallway, dropping all of his equipment, and never taking his eyes off the video camera. All that Jake could say at the time was, "I hope your camera was pointed in the right direction, and saw what I saw!" We all came out of our rooms to see what the commotion was about, except Lisa, who was basically frozen with fear in her room! All that she kept saying was, "Please don't leave me" and "You're freaking me out!"

Once Jake calmed down from his excitement, he relayed what he saw. Jake said he was sitting on the floor waiting for something to happen and glanced to his right toward the video camera when he saw a dark figure standing right next to the camera. It was standing only about 10 feet away from him! It was pretty dark in the hallway, but the soft glow from the viewfinder sent an eerie light across the wall, which enabled Jake to see the figure. Jake stated the figure turned and took off down the main hallway toward the west wing. That's when Jake sprang to his feet. Jake stated if he didn't know any better, he would swear that it was me who was standing next to the camera! (See Figure 34)

We reviewed the video at the time, but we did not capture the apparition. Damn! We surely captured Jake's reaction, though. We all had a good laugh! There's no doubt I would have reacted the same way, but I probably would have ended up peeing in my pants!

We decided to put the video camera inside the small room so it would look down the east wing hallway. We were hoping the apparition would come back, and that we would capture it on the video. This time Kathy and Lisa went to the far end of the east wing, and I went to the end of the main hallway, and sat on the floor. Jake moved to the main hallway also so he would not block the view of Kathy and Lisa at the end of the hallway. After several minutes we heard a strange noise coming from the room the video camera was in. The noise sounded like the video camera was rewinding. I went to check the camera, and discovered it had stopped recording. I

Figure 34 - Jake describing the apparition he saw standing to the right of the video camera

hit the record button, and left the room to go sit back down in the hallway. Again we heard the same noise coming from the room where we placed the video camera. I went back into the room, and discovered the camera stopped recording again! Hmmm, what was going on here? We have never had this problem with the video camera before during an investigation. I started the recording again, and again left the room. This time I stood nearby, and again the camera stopped recording! This was crazy, and was surely no malfunction with the video camera. It appeared that something or someone was shutting the camera off. Again I hit record, but this time I stood right next to the camera to see if it would shut off again. It never did.

While all this was happening to the video camera, Kathy and Lisa were having activity of their own at the end of the east wing hallway. They were using a KII EMF meter, which detects the EMF in the area, along with an IR video camera, and a "Ghost Radar." A "Ghost Radar" is an entertainment app that you can download to your smartphone or tablet that allegedly allows the user to communicate with ghosts and spirits. It is sort of like a Spirit Box or Ovilus in that it will generate and display random words. I do not take the Ghost Radar seriously, and only use it in conjunction with other equipment. The majority of the time, the words have no meaning and do not correspond to any particular question or location, but on rare occasions, the words that are generated can be uncannily accurate. This is just what happened during Kathy and Lisa's investigation down the hallway.

Kathy and Lisa were experiencing electrically charged feelings over their entire bodies, at the same time the KII meter was going crazy, flashing all the way up to red, which indicated there was a lot of electrical energy in the area. The Ghost Radar was spewing out a lot of words, but none of them made any sense. Lisa even captured a ghostly mist that zoomed across her IR video camera. The activity went on for about 15 minutes when all of a sudden the Ghost Radar said "Done." It was then that all of the activity stopped. The feelings went away. The KII readings stayed at a steady green. The Ghost Radar quit spewing out words. All was now calm and quit. Kathy and Lisa stayed there for another 15 minutes to see if the activity would start up again, but it never did. Also, the video camera never shut off again while I was standing next to it. Unfortunately, we did not capture the activity that Kathy and Lisa were experiencing because of the problem with the video camera shutting off. It almost seems that the apparition Jake saw was in the process of stopping the video recording when Jake first saw him. When we put the video camera in the small room, there was no one who had a direct view of the camera, so the apparition was able to stop the recording again and again. Crazy as it sounds, that was the only explanation we could think of.

That was all the activity we had that first night, but we did capture a few EVPs when we reviewed our audio and video. We always captured EVPs at Madison Seminary.

One of the EVPs captured was at the end of the investigation, when Jake and Lisa were gathering up their equipment from the third floor. Jake said to Lisa, "That's all I got." Right after Jake said this, a male's voice on the recording said, "That's all."

This place was so cool and had so much activity that we went back a month later in September 2011. This time even crazier things happened!

This time it was Jake, Kathy, Todd and myself. Lisa wasn't able to make this investigation.

Like the previous investigation, we split up into two teams with Jake and Todd forming one, and Kathy and I making up the other team. We took turns investigating different parts of the buildings with no personal experiences to report. We then joined up as a group, and decided to go into the basement of the original Madison Seminary to see if anything would happen there. We entered the one small room that we called the "Doll Room." The room was pretty bare except for a couple of chairs, a mattress leaning up against a wall, a child's doll and a little toy dog. There were also two windows in the room.

The doll was about three feet tall, and wearing a dress that was black on top and pink with flowers on the bottom and black shoes (See Figure 35). She also had red hair flowing down the middle of her back. The doll appeared to be damaged, too. There was cellophane tape wrapped around her neck, which seemed to be holding her head onto her body.

The little toy dog was a small Dalmatian, like one of the puppies from Disney's movie *101 Dalmatians*. It was wearing a red collar with a red leash attached.

We heard rumors that the doll, which stands on its own, moves about the buildings on her own. Dolls are creepy enough during the day, but one that moves on its own throughout a haunted building? No freaking way! I'm glad I wasn't there by myself!

Figure 35 - The Madison Seminary Doll

When we entered the room, we noticed that the doll was standing in a corner with the toy dog at her feet. I decided to move them apart to see if we would get any type of paranormal reaction. I moved the doll farther down the wall, and moved the dog into the middle of the room. The doll's head fell off when I moved her. I hope that didn't piss her off!

Kathy sat in the cushioned chair while Jake walked around the room using his Cell Sensor EMF meter. Todd was filming with a shoulder-mounted video camera, and I was also walking around the room, monitoring some of the equipment we had set out and taking digital photographs (See Figure 36). A Cell Sensor EMF detector has a large, flashing red light on top, along with a loud, corresponding beeping sound when any EMF is detected (See Figure 37).

While Jake was walking around the room, the Cell Sensor started to go crazy. It was constantly registering a high EMF field no matter where Jake was in the room. A couple of the other EMF meters we had in the room also detected an EMF field, but not as much as the Cell Sensor. When we previously investigated this same room just a few short weeks ago, we did not detect any EMF fields. Now, here

Figure 36 - Todd, Jake and Kathy investigating the "Doll' Room. Notice the doll and the toy dog

it was going off like crazy! We had no explanation as to what would cause it to go off like this, nor could we find any reason within the room.

Jake walked slowly around the room to see if he could find the source of the high EMF. Then, out of the darkness, we all heard what sounded like a dog whimper four times. All of us froze, and then said in unison, "Did you hear that!?!?" The only thing I could say

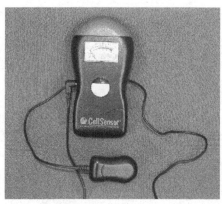

Figure 37 - Cell Sensor EMF Meter

was, "Holy shit!" We knew it came from the middle of the room where the toy dog was sitting on the floor. The whimpers were very distinct and there was no doubt in our minds it came from the toy dog. We all starting talking in amazement. It definitely sounded like the toy dog was whimpering, but how could that be? I then tried to see

if I could get the dog to whimper again. I picked up the toy and examined it. It looked like a child's toy to me. I placed it back on the floor and started pushing it with my hand back and forth across the floor. Nothing. Apparently the dog doesn't do anything, but it had to. We all heard it. We were discussing what we heard, when out of the blue, the dog started barking the children's song B-I-N-G-O! We stood there with our jaws hanging to the floor, and our eyes wide open. We now knew it was definitely coming from the dog! "It's coming from the dog!" I yelled out. Then as quickly as it started, it all stopped. There was no more high EMF in the room, and the dog stopped barking. Everything was quiet. In fact, the EMF was so strong earlier that it "fried" the Cell Sensor, and it was useless the rest of the investigation.

I had to find out more about this toy dog, so I found Tom, the manager of Madison Seminary. I asked him if he knew anything about the dog. Now understand, Tom is inside the building a lot, especially during the investigations. When I asked him if he ever heard the toy dog in the doll room barking or whimpering, he said, "No." He had no idea it could do anything like that. How puzzling!

The next day after the investigation, I did research on the Internet to find out more about the toy dog. I discovered it was made by Fisher Price and is considered a vintage pull toy. It requires three AAA batteries, and when you pull it along the floor, it will bark, whimper and sing a song (See Figure 38).

During the investigation, we checked to see if there were batteries in the toy. There were, but we did not know how old they were. Even when we rolled it across the floor, it still didn't make a sound. We still don't have an answer to this day why the toy acted the way it did. One possible answer was the high EMF in the room. Could it affect the dog in such a way that it could

Figure 38 - Fisher Price Pull Toy like the one in the doll room

whimper and bark, even with old batteries and no one touching it? Maybe the dog was sad when I moved it away from the doll? It's yet another mystery in the world of investigating the paranormal.

I had one more experience at Madison Seminary that really scared the hell out of me. It was in August 2014, and was my sixth time investigating there.

It was about 1:50 a.m. My wife Kathy and I were investigating the same "Doll Room" we investigated during the previous story. This time, there were four chairs in the room, the mattresses leaning up against the wall and two benches. The doll was no longer there. She was in another area of the building. Hopefully she didn't walk there on her own! The toy dog was still in the room. We set up a stationary video camera, a flashlight, two KII EMF Meters, a Mel-meter with a built-in REM Pod and a Natural Tri-Field Meter. Kathy was also listening in real time to her Zoom H4n Digital Audio Recorder with Bose over-the-ear headphones. If anything was going to happen, we were ready.

The room was dark except for some ambient light shining in through the windows. We were conducting an EVP session when we started hearing footsteps walking toward us. It sounded like the steps were walking over some paint chips that had fallen on the floor. The footsteps were fairly loud and seemed to stop when they were next to me. I had the strongest feeling that someone or something was standing right alongside of me! I immediately turned on my flashlight expecting to see some rotting, smiling corpse standing next to me. I was almost frozen with fear as I shined my flashlight around the room trying to find out what was walking around, but just as usual, there was nothing there.

Kathy instinctively raised her feet off the floor, thinking it might be a mouse. If it was a mouse, it had to have been as large as a dog!

After my fears subsided, I rose from my chair and searched the small room for any type of animal that could have caused the footsteps. I looked behind the mattresses since that is where the footsteps seemed to originate, but I could not find any animals hiding there. We could not find any animals anywhere, and besides, there was no place for them to hide (See Figure 39).

Figure 39 – The footsteps walked over the paint chips visible to the right

We then tried recreating the footsteps by having me walk over the paint chips. Bingo (No pun intended!), the footsteps sounded exactly the same! I was happy we captured the footsteps on both the stationary video camera and the digital audio recorder.

Madison Seminary has been the most exciting and productive place I have ever investigated. I am still trying to find that one haunted location that will top all of the evidence and experiences I have had there. The aforementioned experiences are not the only ones we have experienced at Madison Seminary. There have been numerous other minor personal experiences, along with several awesome EVPs captured. So, if you're brave enough, I dare you to spend one night at the Madison Seminary!

For more information on Madison Seminary, please visit their Facebook page.

CHAPTER NINE

PROSPECT PLACE:

PAIN ON THE UNDERGROUND RAILROAD

The old brick mansion known as Prospect Place[36] is located in the tiny village of Trinway, Ohio, which is about 50 miles east of Columbus. Prospect Place is a 29-room mansion built in 1856 by abolitionist George W. Adams. The mansion was an important stop on the Underground Railroad for hundreds of slaves making their way to Canada. The Underground Railroad operation conducted by G. W. Adams and his brother Edward was a huge undertaking. The brothers operated a flouring mill on the Ohio and Erie Canal, and owned warehouses, a boat yard and cooper shops in Dresden, Ohio. When men from the Adams Company would take flour to New Orleans, Louisiana, they would return with runaway slaves hidden beneath the decks of their boats.

The first time I saw Prospect Place, it filled me with a sense of wonder and excitement. I thought to myself, is that where I'm spending the night? I think that a lot when I investigate a new place! This place is so cool looking, like something from an old Alfred Hitchcock movie or any horror movie, as a matter of fact (See Figure 40). I can just imagine "Leatherface" running out the front door with his chainsaw chasing after some helpless victim!

The mansion sits on a small rise on the property, approximately 375 feet from the small, two-lane road and is built entirely from brick. Inside it is divided into two parts. The main part of the mansion is located in the front, and is square in shape, with three floors and a cupola in the middle of the roof. The back half of the mansion is square in shape also, but with only two floors. From the cupola one could see for miles in all directions. It was used to watch for any

Figure 40 – Prospect Place

bounty hunters that might be prowling the countryside searching for runaway slaves. Behind the mansion sits a large three-story, brick barn, which was used to house the horses, carriages, hay and ranch hands.

There are several ghost stories that are told about Prospect Place. There is the tale of a bounty hunter who was hanged in the barn. The legend goes that the bounty hunter came to the house looking for runaway slaves. When told there were none he left, and made camp a short distance away. During the night, ranch hands abducted him and brought him to the barn where they hanged him.

100

There is also the sad story of a little girl who fell to her death from a second-floor balcony. Because of the frozen ground at the time of her death, her body was kept in the basement until the ground was soft enough to allow her a proper burial.

The refuge in the basement is a tale of a female slave who died there from injuries she received on her journey north to freedom.

Lastly, there is the story of the servant in the back stairwell. His primary complaint in life seemed to be his lack of enthusiasm in climbing the many stairs on a daily basis. I don't think he was a happy person.

It is said that these ghosts still roam the mansion and the property to this day. We hoped to meet some of them during our investigation.

The first time we investigated Prospect Place in July of 2007 was not a very good first time experience. Our group reserved the mansion for a private overnight ghost hunt where we would also sleep after the investigation. My wife Kathy, daughter Allison and her boyfriend at the time, my son Andrew, and several other friends and investigators took the trip with us. When we arrived, we discovered several tents around the mansion. It looked like there were several groups of people camping. George Adams, the owner, stated he forgot there was going to be another group camping on the grounds that night. He did explain they would not be going inside the building, but they were camped right next to the mansion. This created a problem for us as any evidence we may capture would have to be thrown out because of possible outside contamination. We were not very happy about this situation, especially since we drove almost two and a half hours, covering about 110 miles. George was very understanding and felt bad about the situation. To make it up to our group, he invited us back at a later date free of charge. We took him up on his offer, and decided to investigate anyway since we were already there. George made it a point to let the campers know there was a paranormal group inside the mansion, and explained to them that the noise needed to be kept to a minimum.

So we set out to investigate the mansion the best we could under the circumstances. We investigated for several hours, but the noise coming from the outside was too loud for us to do a proper investigation. So after some discussion, we all decided to leave and drive back home.

I did have one personal experience during this investigation that was not paranormal, but scared the crap out of me anyways! During an investigation I have never really been frightened by any ghosts or spirits I have encountered. (Except for the one incident at Madison Seminary mentioned earlier!) I do have to say, though, it is the normal and natural things and noises that can scare the crap out of you! Like other investigators, spider webs and loud noises, just to name a few. That is exactly what happened to me while I was investigating the basement.

The basement at Prospect Place is a maze of corridors and rooms with a dirt floor throughout. This is the area where runaway slaves were hidden on the Underground Railroad on their long journey to freedom in Canada. It is not a very pleasant place to investigate, let alone hide and live down there, but it was probably a hundred times better here than their previous circumstances.

I was investigating the basement with my wife Kathy and another investigator friend Steven. Kathy and Steven were doing an EVP session in one of the many rooms while I was videotaping them. They were not having much luck, so I decided to walk around the basement on my own to see if I could capture or witness anything paranormal. I walked into another room across the corridor, and started slowly turning around in the center of the room, quietly videotaping every wall and corner. The room was completely dark except for the night vision in the viewfinder. It was so quiet and still you could hear a mouse creeping along the dirt floor. All of a sudden, there was a large crash directly above me that shattered the quietness. I literally jumped out of my skin and then froze with fear- only for just a second though! I quickly decided I was not in a very good place, and with undue haste, quickly made my exit out of the room and into the room where I knew there were living, breathing people! I told Kathy and Steven what happened, and they quickly called me chicken! I'll show them! I timidly tip-toed back to the room from whence I just previously retreated to show them I wasn't a chicken after all. I was going to figure out what that loud crash was even if it killed me. Wait a minute! What did I just say?! I gingerly stepped into the room ready to flee again at a moment's notice. After I stepped into the room, I listened intently and could faintly hear people talking from the floor above. I went upstairs to see what was going on, and see if they did anything to cause the loud crash I heard. Now I had a legitimate excuse to get out of that room. They can't call me chicken now. Sure enough, my daughter and her boyfriend were in the parlor located directly above the room I was in. I asked them if they did anything to make a loud noise. Allison said she dropped her bracelet on the floor. I told them what happened and how she almost killed her father. We all joked and laughed about it, but at least it wasn't some angry, pissed-off spirit who wanted to kill me. At least I solved that mystery. I think I did subtract at least three years off my life, though. For future investigations I think I'll start using another piece of paranormal equipment —"Depends" underwear!

After reviewing what little audio and video recording we did have, we discovered one possible EVP. This EVP was captured in the basement where it is alleged the female slave died. The only investigators in the basement at the time were my wife Kathy, my daughter Allison and Allison's boyfriend. On the audio, you can hear Kathy and Allison talking about all the noise, and footsteps coming from above them on the second floor. Kathy then said, "If you would like to make your presence known…" At that moment, a male's whispery voice can be heard saying what sounds like, "Help meee." Kathy continues, saying, "Please make a noise down here in the basement." None of the investigators acknowledged the voice, and in fact, never heard it at the time, which is always the case with EVPs. If you hear a voice and can determine it wasn't from a living person, it is called a disembodied voice. The EVP was captured both on the video recorder and the audio recorder. However, the voice seemed closer to the audio recorder (See Figure 41).

We were able to capture something we believed was paranormal, so it doesn't look like it was a wasted trip after all. Yet our next investigation at Prospect Place was a little bit more than we bargained for! The ghosts and spirits would be waiting for us to return.

Our next overnight investigation at Prospect Place took place three months later in October 2007. It was almost the same group of friends and investigators this time, except for two changes. Allison's boyfriend did not make the trip this time. However, my other daughter Amy did, which made a total of 11 investigators for this trip.

The place still filled me with awe as we pulled up the driveway. When we arrived, we discovered that we were going to be the only ones there. Yay! This time it was going to be a cool investigation as there would be no outside interference from campers. I couldn't wait to start investigating.

After we met with George, the owner and caretaker, we proceeded to our bedrooms.

Figure 41 – Kathy doing an EVP session in the basement

There was one bedroom on the first floor in the back of the mansion where two investigators stayed. The rest of us stayed in the two bedrooms on the second floor at the front of the mansion. The bedrooms were pretty nice with several beds and furnishings in each room. My family of five, including myself, took one bedroom, and the other four investigators took the room across the hall. Everyone was in a good mood, and I could tell this was going to be a great night.

Prior to the investigation, all of us went into the village for dinner. After dinner, we returned to Prospect Place to start the investigation. We split up into teams and started the investigation. The team I was on consisted of Kathy, Allison and our friend Steven. We began our investigation in the basement around 9:00 p.m. The last time we investigated the basement, we captured the "Help meee" EVP, and I had my little run-in with Allison's bracelet crashing to the floor.

We walked down the stairs into the dark, dirty and dusty basement. When walking around down there, you just have to wonder what the slaves went through, and what they were thinking while hiding down there. Would they ever make it to freedom? Would they be captured, and taken back to their master, where they would await certain punishment, if not death? Would they die or get injured along the way? Would they ever see their loved ones again? The extreme emotions they went through—apprehension, excitement, fear, pain and sorrow—would surely leave an imprint on this place.

We walked into the room where the remnants of a sealed-up well were located. This is the room where legend tells us that the body of the little girl who fell to her death was kept, until the ground was soft enough to properly bury her (See Figure 42).

We investigated the basement for a little while longer with no personal experiences or anything that we would consider paranormal. We then proceeded up to the second floor where we

Figure 42 – The sealed-up well in the basement

started to investigate one of the rooms towards the back of the mansion. The time now was about 10:20 p.m. I was the first to enter the room and immediately backed out because of the strong energy I felt coming from inside the room. It was the feeling of walking into some type of electrical force field. My whole body started to tingle with every one of my hairs standing at attention. After the feeling dissipated, we all entered the room and started to walk around. As I walked to the middle of the room, it felt as if I walked through a giant spider web! I would have sworn that the whole left side of my face was covered in a spider's silky web. I immediately called out that I just went through a spider web, and for someone to check my face with a flashlight and to start taking photographs. My daughter ran over and shined her flashlight on my face, while Steven started taking pictures. Like usual, there was nothing there (See Figure 43). Thank God for that because I am extremely afraid of spiders. You could definitely say I have an intense case of arachnophobia!

I remember the day working as a police officer when I received a call of some teenagers partying in the woods. I drove to the area, parked my patrol car and started walking quietly through the woods to sneak up on them. I loved sneaking up on people and was pretty good at it. I

Figure 43 – Allison checking my face for spider webs

enjoyed seeing their expressions when they turned around and saw me standing behind them! The route I took did not have any paths, so I had to walk through the underbrush and bushes. All of a sudden, without any warning, I walked through this HUGE spider web! I immediately started flailing my arms and beating myself all over my body! I knew there had to be a giant spider trapped somewhere in my uniform! There were plenty of places for it to hide since I was also wearing my gun belt. So much for trying to sneak up stealthily on a group of teenagers. I'm pretty sure they saw this crazy cop dancing in the woods for no apparent reason, laughing all the way as they fled the woods. At least they had a good laugh at my expense! "Ah, 712 to dispatch, back in the car. No signs of those teenagers. I'll be returning to station." Mission aborted. When I arrived at the station, I went into the bathroom and took everything off just to make sure it wasn't still on me. Let me say that it was one LONG-ass drive back to the station!

This was the longest time I have ever felt the spider web sensation during an investigation. Other times, the feeling was only there for a moment, but this time it felt like something was holding my face and was not going to let go. It seemed like the feeling lasted about a minute before the sensation finally went away. I was like, "Holy shit! There is definitely something going on in this room."

Like mentioned earlier, some paranormal investigators, myself included, believe that if a ghost or spirit touches you, it will feel like a spider web. Obviously, there is no proof to support this theory. It is just one of the many mysteries in a long line of unanswered questions when it comes to investigating the paranormal.

We stayed in the room a bit longer conducting EVP sessions, but just like other times, things quieted down. It's like they play a cat and mouse game with you. I wonder if they sit back with all their other ghost friends saying, "Did you see the look on that guy's face when I touched it?!?"

We then headed toward the back servant area when we were contacted by other investigators, advising me that my other daughter Amy, was sick. We proceeded down to the first floor, and went into the parlor where we found Amy sitting on a couch. All of the other investigators were gathered around her with concerned looks on their faces. Amy seemed to be really out of it. She was sweating, felt cold and clammy to the touch, and her eyes were rolling back in her head. It seemed like she was going in and out of consciousness (See Figure 44). Amy said she felt nauseated and extremely weak. She became so disoriented and lethargic that we were getting ready to call an ambulance. We removed her from the room she was in, and all of a sudden, she just snapped out of it. That was really strange. Did she just become possessed? Guess we'll have to watch her, and make sure her head doesn't spin around and that she doesn't throw up split pea soup!

Figure 44 – Allison and Kathy checking on Amy

Amy was not the type of person to freak out like that. Sure, she was afraid to watch scary movies or go to "haunted houses," the kind that pop up everywhere during the Halloween season. However, she was not afraid of the paranormal. There were times when we stayed and investigated real haunted inns and hotels and Amy would end up sleeping in a room by herself with no complaints or fears at all.

After we made sure Amy was okay, we went back upstairs to the second floor where we left off. This time we entered the very back room of the mansion. Once we entered, my other daughter Allison started complaining about her stomach burning. She stated, "My stomach's like burning. It feels like it's on fire." We asked her to lift up her jacket to show her stomach. We then shined a flashlight on her stomach. Across her abdomen, clear as day, there appeared to be three to four horizontal welts or scratches (See Figure 45). What the hell's going on! First Amy and now Allison! We could not believe what we were seeing. We thought there had to be a logical explanation for the scratches. Allison started getting really scared. First her sister Amy becoming sick and now this. We told her the marks were probably creases in her abdomen from bending over while she was sitting on the ground earlier. She did not buy that explanation because, as she said, if that were the case, why does the area burn? She was right, and we were perplexed because we could not figure out how the scratches got there. Allison, with a worried look on her face, stated, "I don't like it here anymore." It was only a little after 11:00 p.m. and we still had the whole night to go.

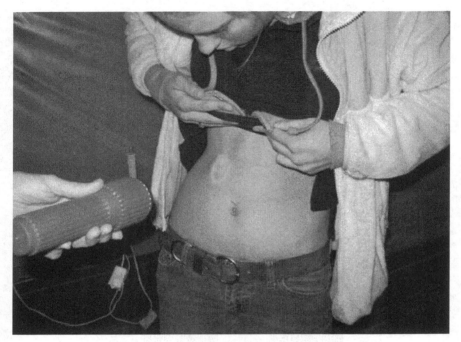

Figure 45 – Scratches on Allison's abdomen

Could the ghost of the servant in the stairwell have caused the scratches? Was the servant angry because we were invading its home or was it just trying to make its presence known? Obviously, there is no way to know for sure.

Both Amy and Allison eventually recovered from their personal experiences, so we continued investigating until about 3:00 a.m. We set up some stationary video cameras throughout the mansion, and then got ready for bed. After a decent night's sleep, we all woke up in the morning, packed up all of our equipment and left Prospect Place to head home.

There were no other personal experiences during the night or while we were sleeping. A review of all the video and audio revealed nothing else extraordinary.

Investigators and paranormal enthusiasts can still spend the night at Prospect Place, but according to Allison and Amy, do it at your own risk!

For more information on Prospect Place, please visit their website at www.gwacenter.org.

CHAPTER TEN

MAPLE HEIGHTS, OHIO:

MY VERY OWN HAUNTED HOUSE

As I stated in Chapter 1, I was not one of the "lucky" people who grew up in a haunted house or had a lot of paranormal experiences. In a way, I would always get jealous and envious when someone talked about the haunted house they grew up in. How I wish I could have lived in a haunted house. What am I thinking? That would all change in the spring of 1998 when I purchased a home in Maple Heights, Ohio, and got my wish.

I believe I mentioned in an earlier chapter that 1997 and 1998 were both rough years for me as I was going through a divorce at the time. It wasn't a terrible divorce like some of the divorce horror stories I've heard about, but it was still a tough time for me. My ex-wife and I did get along well for the sake of our children. Allison was 8 years old at the time, Amy was 7 and Andrew was 4. It was tough for me because I would not be able to see them as much as I wanted. Every Wednesday and every other weekend wasn't nearly enough time with them, especially since I just purchased a house and would be pretty much living alone now. During the divorce, my cousin and his wife graciously allowed me to live with them until I purchased my own home.

I moved into my new house in May 1998, and strange things started to happen within the first month living there. Well, it wasn't a new home, but it was new to me.

The house I purchased was a small Cape Cod-style bungalow built in 1954. The house totaled 1,161 square feet and consisted of a partially finished basement, along with a kitchen, living room, two bedrooms and a full bathroom on the first floor. The second floor had hardwood floors throughout and consisted of a large bedroom and a half bathroom.

I purchased the home from the estate of the previous owner who passed away in July of 1997. After some online research, I discovered that she was 72 years old when she passed. I also found out that she passed away in a hospital, and not in the bedroom I would be sleeping in. Let's just call her Eleanor[†]. I could not locate any information on her husband other than that he passed away in 1987. I don't know if he passed away in the house or somewhere else. I did find out that they purchased the house in 1975, and Eleanor lived there for 22 years.

It didn't take long for things to start happening. The first thing that happened in the house really freaked me out at the time. I made my bedroom in one of the rooms on the first floor. I was kind of nervous about making my bedroom on the second floor because there were several locks on the *outside* of the door, as if the previous owner was trying to keep something locked up that she did not want to get out. I know there probably was a logical reason, but I've always had an over-imagination. One night I went to bed and as I lay there I could hear soft whispering in the room. The whispers became louder whenever I put my ear to the pillow. It sounded like someone was underneath the bed whispering. I imagined that there were small creatures under the bed making plans to get me during the night. Yes, I watched too much television, and kept thinking about the little

---

[†] Name changed

creatures from the movie, *Don't Be Afraid of the Dark*[37] and the Zuni fetish doll from the third segment of *Trilogy of Terror*.[38] My mind was going crazy, but where was the whispering coming from?! I lifted my head off the pillow, and scanned around the dark room waiting for my eyes to adjust. You have to understand that after 40 years of living with family, this would be my first time living alone, and this was not a good start. Hmmm, the whispering diminished. Maybe it was just my imagination. Yet, as soon as I laid my head on the pillow, it would start up again. It was almost like they were watching me, and waiting for me to lay back down before whispering about their horrible plans. Whenever I lifted my head off the pillow, the whispering would stop. I started getting scared shitless! Were my ears playing tricks on me? What the hell was going on? I thought there had to be a logical explanation for what I was hearing. I laid my head back on my pillow, and listened more closely. It was definitely someone talking softly, so I got up and walked around the room searching for anything. Then I noticed out my window that my neighbors' had their television on. The houses were fairly close together, and I could see the soft blue glow coming from their window. That was it! It was their television I was hearing. For whatever reason, my pillow was acting like a conduit. Whenever I laid my head down, I could hear their television. I couldn't make out exactly what they were saying, but I now knew it was definitely the cause of what I was hearing. Whew, that was a close one! I surely thought I was going to be dragged down some unseen hole to the darkest depths of who knows what! Yea, I do have an imagination. This also illustrates a point that not all things you think are paranormal are actually paranormal.

I started to feel comfortable in the house, but I was still lonely. I guess that's why my children gave me two kittens to give me company. We named them Abbott and Costello. Strange things continued to happen in the house, but not on a frequent basis.

There were several times when I would come home from work, to discover the thermostat in the hallway turned all the way up. At first I thought it could have been one of the cats jumping up, and changing the setting. But then I thought there's no way they could have jumped that high. The thermostat was five feet off the ground, and to have it happen on several occasions? Could Eleanor have been cold, and turned up the heat to keep warm?

I made the second floor into my children's bedroom and play area for when they would come over every other weekend. I always kept the door shut up there, and had no reason to go up there unless they were there. But on a couple occasions I would arrive home from work, and the lights would be on in their room. I know there was no way the cats could open the door, turn on the lights, and then close the door. Turning on the thermostat - maybe. Cats are smart, but not that smart. I would check the house, and upstairs to make sure nothing was amiss or missing. It seemed more logical to think that someone broke into the house, than to believe ghosts were turning on lights. However, the house would still be locked up and there would be no signs of forced entry into the house. It was strange, but none of it scared me – well maybe the whispering!

Every once in a while my children would say they didn't like sleeping upstairs because they thought it was haunted. I asked them what they meant. They said it sounds like someone was walking around their bedroom at night. I told them it was probably the floorboards creaking and settling since it was an old house. I was soon to find out different.

After those few minor incidents, things began to quiet down for the most part. Or maybe it was because I wasn't paying attention to it anymore. I was finally getting used to the house.

In 2002, Kathy and I got married, and she and her son Dale moved in. After living alone for four years, it was nice living with someone again, even though at that point I didn't mind living by myself.

We moved our master bedroom from the first floor to the second floor because it was a much larger room. The room was large enough that we made half of it into our bedroom, and the other half into a living area, with two recliners, a television and a computer work area.

We moved Allison, Amy and Andrew to the two bedrooms on the first floor. Dale moved into the bedroom in the basement.

Nothing paranormal happened in the house for several years, but in December 2007, things started to pick up, and both Kathy and I started having experiences. Dale had since moved away, joining the United States Marine Corps and eventually getting married.

On December 26 around 2:30 a.m. a strong scent of perfume in our bedroom woke me up. Kathy, being a heavy sleeper, did not wake. I was thinking it was just Eleanor and went back to sleep. I left for work later that morning before Kathy woke up, so I did not have a chance to discuss the perfume with her. Later that day, Kathy called me on the phone and told me she woke up around 7:30 a.m. and smelled a strange perfume. I told her my experience of smelling the perfume earlier that night—just a minor start to some bizarre experiences we would soon be encountering in the house.

Kathy knew about my prior experiences when I first moved into the house. I wanted to make sure she knew she was moving into a possible haunted house. It didn't bother her at all because she was just as interested in the paranormal as I was. In fact, she told me she grew up in a haunted house, and had several personal experiences of her own growing up. Cool!

Together we tried to figure out who or what could have caused some of the stuff that was going on. The only thing we could think of was Eleanor, the previous owner. It was her house for 22 years, and if you believe in ghosts, that would make perfect sense for her to come back. So, whenever something would happen we would say, "That's just Eleanor."

After the perfume smell, we started smelling other pleasant aromas in the house like the smell of brewing coffee when there was no coffee brewing at the time. One night, both of us smelled garlic bread baking in the kitchen, and one early Friday morning, we both smelled the pleasant aroma of pancakes being cooked. If it was Eleanor, it smelled like she was a great cook.

Items were always falling or being knocked over in the house, too. A water glass sitting in a cabinet in the kitchen shattered for no apparent reason. A toy motorcycle that was in Andrew's bedroom fell off a shelf that it was sitting on. A photograph in a frame, sitting on a table, fell onto the floor with no one near it. A children's pool table that was laying on its side in the basement fell over. Something fell behind our headboard while we were sleeping one night, which scared the crap out of us! I got up and searched behind the bed and on the floor, but could find anything that had fallen.

Sometimes items moved around and went missing. One time, my daughter Amy placed her cellphone on the couch in the living room. When she went to get it, she discovered it missing. We searched all over the house, eventually finding it hidden in the cabinet beneath her fish tank in her bedroom.

Other times we would discover a bedroom light on or a basement light on, knowing that all the lights were turned off when we left the house.

Figure 46 – The hallway

There were two primary areas of activity within the house. The hallway on the first floor (See Figure 46) and the master bedroom upstairs (See Figure 47). Some of the scarier incidents seemed to happen after my father passed away in September of 2008.

Numerous times we would be sitting in the living room watching television and would hear someone walking across the hardwood floors upstairs in our master bedroom. During one incident, I was sleeping upstairs in my bed after working the midnight shift. Kathy and Allison were in the living room watching television when they heard me get out of bed, walk across the floor to the computer desk, and slide the chair back. Kathy said to Allison, "Looks like your dad's up." Kathy proceeded upstairs only to find me sound asleep. She came back downstairs and told Allison that I was still sound asleep. Allison's eyes got wide, and she said, "Holy crap!"

In 2009, we had several scary incidents happen in our bedroom. One night, Kathy and I went to bed around 3:00 a.m. We were only in bed for a couple of minutes when both of us heard one of the rocking chairs in the living room portion start rocking back and forth. We could clearly hear the chair as it creaked back and forth, back and forth. We both sat straight up at the same time, saying to each other,

Figure 47 – Master bedroom

"Did you just hear that?!?" We strained our eyes to see through the darkness, but could not see anything sitting in the chair. We knew it wasn't going to hurt us, so we just laid back down and went to sleep.

Another time we went to bed and just started drifting off when we heard something or someone walking around our bed. We could definitely hear the footsteps, especially when the wood floorboards started to creak. Again, we shot straight up, expecting to see someone standing beside our bed, smiling a hideous smile, but just like every other time, there was nothing there.

One time, Kathy heard the footsteps walking around the bed while I was sleeping. She said when it was at the end of the bed, the bed covers started to be pulled off. She grabbed the covers and told it to stop, which it did.

There is a metal laundry chute door in the half bathroom on the second floor that leads down to the basement. Again, one night while we were in bed, it sounded like someone put dirty clothes down the laundry chute because we heard the chute door open then shut.

Numerous times during my law enforcement career I would have to work the midnight shift, which ran from 7:00 p.m. until 7:00 a.m. On my days off, I would stay up to 5:00 a.m., because I wanted to stay on a schedule so I would be awake when I worked. On one of my days off, I was working on the computer in the master bedroom. Kathy was sound asleep in the same room. It was about 3:00 a.m., and the house was quiet except for me typing on the keyboard. The quiet was broken up by someone or something walking up the stairs to our bedroom. I froze with fear with the hair on the back of my neck standing up! "Holy shit," I thought! There was actually something coming up the stairs! I then heard it walking into our bedroom. From where the computer desk was situated, you could not see the door to our bedroom and my back was to the door. After a few steps into our room, it stopped or should I say paused. I was too petrified to turn around for fear of what I might see or not see. I sat there for what seemed liked forever. What was it waiting for? Why didn't it come further into the room? There had been no more footsteps for a while, so I slowly turned around in my chair and got up to look around. There was nothing there, and our bedroom door was still closed. Wow, maybe I should go to bed at a regular time from now on!

We also had a lot of strange things going on in the hallway on the first floor. We would constantly see dark shadows moving in the hallway while we were watching television in the living room. There was no shape to them, just a dark mass that you would see out of the corner of your eye. One time after taking a shower, I opened the bathroom door and started to step into the hallway when a white, misty figure walked in front of me from the left to the right and entered the spare guest bedroom.

Another time, Kathy actually saw a figure of a man standing in the hallway. She was holding our grandson, playing with him by dipping him up and down, and as she came up, she saw a man standing next to her. She remained calm because she didn't want to frighten our grandson. She laid him down in the living room and glanced back, but the figure was gone. She became frightened because she was home alone, and thought someone broke into the house. She called me at work, and told me what she just saw. She searched the house, but could not find anyone else. I reassured her that there was probably no living person in the house, and what she saw was probably a ghost. Some reassurance!

Another incident occurred when Lisa, a friend and fellow paranormal investigator, stayed with us after a late-night investigation. Lisa was sleeping in the spare guest room, the same one the white misty figure walked into. In the early morning, she was awakened by the sound of the doorknob turning. Lisa looked at the doorknob and saw it rattling and moving. She yelled out "Who's there?" No one answered. The knob stopped moving, and all returned quiet. The next morning, Lisa told us what happened, and declared our house is definitely haunted!

One last incident involved Judy, another fellow paranormal investigator and psychic from our team. She stopped over our house on the way to an investigation. After Judy and Kathy left the house, Kathy asked her if she felt anything while in the house. Kathy wanted to know because my father had just passed away a few months earlier, and she wanted to see if he was there, and if Judy picked up on him. Judy said, as a matter of fact, she did pick up on someone in the house. Judy stated when she came out of the bathroom she saw a male figure standing in the hallway. Judy relayed he spoke to her and said, "Another one is moving in." The next day, my daughter Amy was moving in with us on a temporary basis. Judy would not have known this because we had just met her and we never talked with her about this. Kathy showed Judy a recent photograph of my father. Judy acknowledged that was the male figure she saw, but said when she saw him, he looked much younger.

There were a couple of times when I was home by myself working on the computer upstairs and I would hear the side door open. It would then sound like someone was walking around downstairs. Whenever I would go check, there would be no one there.

The last time that happened to me was the night of April 30, 2012. During that evening, I was with Kathy and her family at her sister's house. Kathy's mother was dying and under hospice care. We weren't sure how long she had or if she would make it through the night. Kathy told me to go home, and if anything changed, she would call me. So, reluctantly I left and drove home. When I arrived home, the house was extremely dark and seemed darker than normal. I went upstairs to my bedroom, changed out of my clothes, and climbed into bed. The time was about 11:55 p.m. No sooner did I lay down in bed when I heard the side door open and close. My son Andrew was staying with us at the time, so I thought it was him. I heard a lot of movement and walking around downstairs so I got up, opened the bedroom door, and yelled downstairs for Andrew. It was extremely quiet downstairs. There was a stillness downstairs that you could feel piercing through the darkness. In fact, all of the lights were still off. That was very strange and spooky at the same time. I yelled a second time and still no answer. I closed and locked the bedroom door and looked out the window to see if Andrew's car was parked in the driveway. It was not. Just then, my cellphone rang, and needless to say, it scared the living shit out of me! Complete silence, spooky feelings, blinding darkness, ghost in house, wham

LOUD CELLPHONE! It was my wife Kathy on the other end calling to say her mother just passed away. I told her I know. I think she just visited me to say good-bye.

One of the strange things about living in that house was we never investigated it, and we had a team of investigators that would have jumped at the chance to investigate. I guess we knew it was haunted, and had a good idea of who it was—Eleanor, my dad and now Kathy's mom. We felt at ease in the house and never felt threatened at all. Freaked out a couple times, but never threatened.

We moved from that house in October 2012, not because we were afraid. We just wanted to have our dream house built.

We still own the house and rent it out now. A little while back, my tenant asked me if the house was haunted. She told me her daughter keeps hearing someone walking upstairs on the second floor. I told her, "If I said yes, would you leave?" She said no. At the time of this writing, my tenant and her daughter still live there and, apparently so does Eleanor.

CONCLUSION

Everyone has a ghost story to tell. It seems no matter who I speak with, they all have personal stories to share or something that has happened to them, a friend or family member. The sharing of experiences happens all the time, especially at my lectures.

I believe there are more haunted locations, houses, businesses and buildings in this world than anyone can imagine. It seems the paranormal is now a part of mainstream society. The inundation of all the reality paranormal shows and shows about haunted places have filled our evening viewing pleasures. There seems to be a new paranormal reality show every new television season. Here is a short list of some of the more popular paranormal shows throughout the years, including the year the show first aired and the network.

1959 – One Step Beyond (ABC, TBS)
1976 – In Search Of... (U.S. Syndicated)
1987 – Unsolved Mysteries (NBC, CBS)
1992 – Sightings (Fox, SyFy Syndicated)
1996 – The Unexplained (A&E, Biography)
1997 – Beyond Belief: Fact or Fiction (Fox)
1998 – Haunted History (History, Biography)
2000 – Scariest Places on Earth (ABC Family)
2000 – MTV's Fear (MTV)
2002 – Most Haunted (Living TV, Paranormal Channel, Travel)
2003 – Weird Travels (Travel)
2004 – Ghost Hunters (SyFy)
2005 – A Haunting (Discovery, Destination America)
2006 – Paranormal State (A&E)
2007 – Destination Truth (SyFy)
2008 – Ghost Hunters International (SyFy)
2008 – Ghost Adventures (Travel)
2009 – Ghost Lab (Discovery)
2009 – Celebrity Ghost Stories (Biography, LMN)
2009 – Fact or Faked: Paranormal Files (SyFy)
2010 – My Ghost Story (Biography, LMN)

2011 – Haunted Collector (SyFy)
2012 – The Haunting Of… (Biography)
2013 – When Ghosts Attack (Destination America)
2014 – Ghost Stalkers (Destination America)

The list goes on and on!

See Appendix III for a complete list of all the television shows that have dealt with the paranormal, including ghosts, UFOs, monsters, psychics and everything else weird.

In regard to paranormal television shows, there are some really good ones out there, just as there are some bad ones. It's always interesting to see what gimmick they come up with next.

We've come a long way since the television show *In Search Of…*[39], first aired in 1976 hosted by Leonard Nimoy[40], Mr. Spock from Star Trek. *In Search Of…* was one of the first television shows that dealt with unusual phenomenon, as well as the paranormal. I guess it really wasn't the first show dealing with the paranormal. If you want to get really technical, *Scooby-Doo, Where Are You!*[41], which aired in 1969, was one of the first shows dealing with the paranormal, even though all the paranormal evidence they gathered proved to be fake. "…and I would have gotten away with it too, if it wasn't for you meddling kids."

In my opinion, the problem with some of these television shows and movies is that people take them seriously and as reality. I know there is some good evidence these shows have captured, but I am also sure that a lot of the claims and evidence are exaggerated and/or faked. Most of these television shows, if not all of them, are for entertainment purposes and ratings only.

I remember when the movie *The Exorcist*[42] was released in 1973. Audiences went crazy, sometimes screaming, crying, fainting and running out of the theater believing they were possessed, and they were all perfectly fine prior to going into the theater. If anyone heard any type of noise in their attic, they believed demons had invaded their home. If little Joey talked back, he was possessed. It was mass hysteria.

Movies are a powerful influence on people's everyday lives, and many believe it to be the truth. Case in point. Two of the most iconic Universal Studio's Monsters are Dracula[43] and the Wolf Man.[44] Both are rooted in legend, especially in the European countries. Take Dracula, for example. In Bram Stoker's[45] book *Dracula*, it is never mentioned that sunlight can kill Dracula, nor is it a part of vampire lore. It was Hollywood that first added the sunlight idea in the 1922 movie *Nosferatu.*[46] Other films about Dracula and vampires since ran with the idea that sunlight can kill a vampire. The Wolf Man is another example of Hollywood adding their own ideas to movies to make them more entertaining. In the legends of werewolves, it is never mentioned that a silver bullet can kill the creature, but in the 1941 movie *The Wolf Man* they added the idea that a silver bullet is one of the only ways to kill the beast. All of Hollywood's doing, just like *The Exorcist's* Ouija board mentioned in Chapter Four.

When I first started investigating, I did it more for the excitement and thrill. Although, as I found out, there is not much excitement or thrill in investigating the paranormal. How exciting is it to sit in a darkened rooms for hours, talking to no one, and with no one responding—at least that you can hear? Then you have to sit through hours and hours of audio and video in the slight chance you may have captured a three-second EVP. Don't get me wrong, there are still aspects of investigating that are exciting, like investigating some awesome locations like Waverly Hills Sanatorium[47] in Louisville, Kentucky, or the Farnsworth Inn[48] in Gettysburg, Pennsylvania.

Now that I have been investigating for a while, I don't do it for the excitement or thrill anymore. I do it to help people. That's why we formed Tri-C Ghost Hunters in January 2013. Our mission statement reads, "Our mission is to provide insight and assistance to our clients who are experiencing possible paranormal activity in their lives, homes, or businesses, as well as to the public, based on our knowledge and experience."

Most people experiencing paranormal activity in their home or business don't know where or who to go to for help. That's where a team such as Tri-C Ghost Hunters comes in. Together with the client we can try to figure out what is going on. Some of our clients think they're going crazy and just need someone to confirm what is going on. Hopefully, we can assure them that they are not, and that thousands, if not millions, of people have gone or are going through the same thing they are.

Not every house or business that has strange activity going on is paranormal in nature. A lot of them have natural, logical explanations. Two cases we recently investigated turned out to be nothing paranormal at all.

In November of 2014, we investigated an apartment in Parma Heights, Ohio. The client, who was desperate for help, stated they were seeing shadows in the apartment, and occasionally the lights would dim, and then get bright. Reports of seeing shadows is probably the most common activity that clients report. The most serious aspect of this case, however, was the mother did not feel comfortable in her apartment, especially in her bedroom. She stated she was having difficulty sleeping and was only getting about four or five hours of sleep a night. Her 14-month-old daughter would wake up screaming and crying in the middle of the night for no apparent reason. During our investigation, we entered the daughter's bedroom and were immediately overwhelmed by a strong "energy" that was in the room. I actually started to get a headache, and was also becoming nauseous, as were a couple other investigators. We conducted an EMF sweep in the bedroom and discovered a child's fan sitting on the dresser was emitting an EMF of 171.4 milligauss! EMF readings in the master bedroom reached levels of 60.0-70.0 milligauss! The majority of homes we have investigated generally have readings of 0.0-3.0 milligauss. The readings can get higher near electrical outlets, appliances, electronics, fuse boxes, water lines and anything else that uses electricity or emits a magnetic field, but this was the highest reading we have ever come across during an investigation. No wonder the daughter was waking up screaming, and our client could only sleep four or five hours a night. They were living in what is commonly called in the paranormal field a "fear cage" or "panic room," in which high EMF was affecting their brains. While there is still great controversy, studies have suggested that high doses of EMF can cause hypersensitivity, sleep disturbance, mental confusion, dizziness, headaches, anxiety and fatigue, among other things.

We advised our client to get rid of the fan immediately, which they did. After that, they never had another problem. Our client stated she was now able to sleep and felt comfortable in her apartment again.

Another case we investigated in May of 2015 also turned out not to be paranormal in nature. This case involved a house in North Ridgeville, Ohio. Our client described shadows were being seen and movement was heard throughout the house, among other minor occurrences. From what our client told us, it seemed most of the activity occurred in the kitchen and the basement. When she was in the kitchen she had the feeling of being watched, and had bad feelings when she looked down the steps into the basement. Our client added she did not like the basement, saying it had a sour smell and made her uncomfortable when she was down there. She also complained of feeling nauseated, especially in the basement, and of constantly being sick or getting hurt.

Our team arrived at the house, and after getting a tour of the first and second floors, we entered the basement. In the basement all of us were overcome by a strong natural gas smell. It was so strong and heavy that you could actually see it in the air! We all started to feel ill and immediately left the basement. We advised our client that there was a natural gas leak, and she needed to contact the gas company immediately. We opened all of the windows, then exited the house and waited for the gas company to arrive.

Some symptoms of prolonged natural gas exposure are headaches, fatigue, nausea, confusion, flu-like symptoms and even death.

After a short wait, the gas company employee arrived. We told him about the strong natural gas we smelled in the basement. He checked the basement and kitchen, and discovered a major gas leak coming from the gas oven, which just happened to be right near the steps leading down to the basement. There was also a small gas leak coming from the water heater in the basement. He asked our client if she had been using the oven recently. She said she used it to make dinner earlier. It was so strong in the basement because that is where the gas was settling. No wonder she didn't like the basement! He further stated if the oven was on long enough it would have definitely killed her and her family. The gas company shut off the gas to the oven and water heater, and placed warning signs on the shutoff valves. Prior to us leaving the house, we conducted a sweep with our carbon monoxide detector, just to make sure it was all clear, which it was.

So, as you can see from those two cases, someone who thinks their house is haunted, their strange occurrences are not always paranormal in nature.

We always strive to find the right answers for our clients. Unfortunately, however, we cannot always figure out what is going on in a home or business. We don't always have the answers, though. No one does, but we will continue to help others the best we can. That's why I do what I do and the reason why there is Tri-C Ghost Hunters.

I have learned several things during my years investigating. First - anything can happen at any time. Second - everyone has theories, but no one has definite answers. Third - no investigator, professional or amateur knows everything about the paranormal. Fourth - people in the paranormal field are doing the best they can to come up with answers. Finally, the most important thing I've learned, especially since I am much older now, is to always wear Depends on investigations! Just kidding!

TRI-C GHOST HUNTERS

Tri-C Ghost Hunters is an LLC company that was formed in January of 2013 with 10 original members. My wife Kathy Feketik, Todd Schelat, Jake Tolin and I are the co-founders. We are a team of dedicated paranormal investigators and enthusiasts located in the Cleveland, Canton and Columbus areas of Ohio who investigate claims of paranormal activity throughout Ohio and the surrounding states.

Our team consists of investigators, tech specialists, audio specialists, researchers and psychics/mediums. We have come together as a team to share our experiences and expertise in investigating the paranormal, and to give our clients the best they can possibly receive through investigations and research of their homes and businesses.

At the time of this writing, we have over 30 members, which includes regular-full time members and auxiliary members.

We currently have over 140 years' total experience in investigations and the paranormal, in general. As individual investigators, we have been on over 725 total investigations, from a small two-bedroom apartment in West Virginia to a large 12th century castle in Scotland.

We use a wide variety of equipment during our investigations, everything from pendulums to a Flir thermal imager, in an attempt to gather data and evidence to prove or disprove if the home or business is experiencing true paranormal activity. The most important thing we bring to an investigation though is our common sense. In some cases, there can be a reasonable and logical explanation for what is occurring, as was mentioned earlier.

We do not ask for any money or donations for any investigation. All of our investigations are free of charge. Each member purchases his or her own equipment, and pays for any travel that may be required.

The safety and well-being of our clients is of the utmost importance. Therefore, all of our full-time regular investigators are required to have criminal background checks before they are allowed to investigate any private home or business.

We are here because we want to help you figure out what is going on in your home or business.

Tri-C Ghost Hunters also conducts presentations on investigating the paranormal. The presentation includes audio, video and photographic evidence from past cases, as well as the basics of conducting an investigation, and the equipment used.

If you are interested in a presentation for your library, school, business or any other organization, please contact me through my e-mail or our website.

Please make sure to check us out on our website for up-to-date information on current members, investigations and events.

Please like and follow us on Facebook and Twitter.

www.tcghohio.org

Appendix I

DEFINITIONS

AFTERLIFE - Life after our physical body dies.

AGENT - A living person who is the focus of poltergeist activity, typically a teenage female.

ANGEL - Messengers of God who can also protect and guide human beings.

ANNIVERSARY IMPRINT - An imprint that usually manifests around the same time each year.

ANOMALY - Something that is out of place and unexplained.

APPARITION - A disembodied soul or spirit that can be seen visually.

APPORT - A physical object that can materialize and appear at will, and can include coins, watches, jewelry and even food.

ARTEFACT - Term used to describe the slight noises or residual images produced by the internal mechanisms of equipment which could be misinterpreted as paranormal sounds or images.

ASTRAL BODY - The body that a person occupies during an out-of-body experience.

ASTRAL PLANE - A world that is believed to exist above our physical world.

ASTRAL PROJECTION - The conscious initiation of an out-of-body experience.

AUDIO VOICE PHENOMENON (AVP) - Disembodied voices that are heard at the time of the investigation, and may or may not be recorded on electronic devices.

AURA - A field of energy that emanates from matter. It is especially prominent around living things.

AUTOMATIC WRITING - A method used by spirit mediums to obtain information from the "other side."

BANISHING - Procedure to cast a paranormal entity from a location.

BANSHEE - A death omen or spirit that attaches itself to certain families.

BENIGN SPIRIT - A spirit that is harmless or has no ill intentions.

BILOCATION - A phenomenon where a person seems to be at more than one location at the same time. (See doppelganger)

CHANNELING - In this method of spirit communication, a spirit will pass information directly to a medium or channeler who will then relay the information to others.

CLAIRAUDIENCE - Hearing voices, astral music or discarnate beings.

CLAIREOFACTOR - To have an extraordinary sense of smell, as if you could smell flowers before they bloom or smell trouble before it happens or death before it occurs.

CLAIRSENTIENCE - The ability to clearly feel yours and/or another's emotions and sensations.

CLAIRVOYANCE - The ability to obtain knowledge based on unexplainable intuition, vision or psychic senses.

CLEARING - Ridding a location of ghostly activity.

COLD SPOTS - Patches of cool/cold air strewn about haunted locations.

COLLECTIVE APPARITION - A type of ghost sighting that occurs when one or more people see the same apparition.

CRISIS APPARITION - An apparition that is seen when a person is seriously ill, seriously injured or at the point of death.

DEBUNK - To show or prove something as false.

DEMATERIALIZATION - The sudden disappearance of a person or spirit in full view of witnesses.

DEMON - Fallen angels under the command of Satan.

DEMONOLOGIST - One who studies and practices the art of demonology. An individual who specializes in the removal of evil or demonic forces from a given environment using the art of demonology.

DEMONOLOGY - The study of demons or beliefs about demons.

DIRECT WRITING - Where spirits actually communicate by the use of writing.

DISEMBODIED - Having no physical body.

DISEMBODIED VOICE - A voice that is heard with human ears whose source comes from someone without a physical body.

DIVINING/DOWSING RODS - A forked rod from a tree said to indicate the presence of water or minerals underground. May also indicate an energy field. Can also be made of metal.

DOPPELGANGER - A ghost of the present that looks identical to a living person, but behaves differently.

DOUBLE - A ghost of the present that looks identical to a living person, and behaves identically.

DIVINATION/DOWSING - Interpreting the motions of rods, sticks, pendulums and other such instruments to obtain information (also called diving).

DIRECT VOICE PHENOMENON (DVP) - An auditory "spirit" voice that is spoken directly to the sitter's at a séance.

EARTHBOUND - Refers to a ghost that is unable to cross over at the time of death.

ECTOPLASM - A substance that allegedly oozes from ghosts or spirits and makes it possible for them to materialize and perform feats of telekinesis.

ELECTROMAGNETIC FIELD (EMF) - A physical field produced by electrically charged objects. It affects the behavior of charged objects in the vicinity of the field.

ELECTRONIC VOICE PHENOMENON (EVP) - Disembodied voices or sounds that are captured on recording (audio or video) devices.

ELEMENTALS - A term used to describe angry or malicious spirits. Also known as "earth spirits."

EMF DETECTOR - An instrument for measuring the magnitude and direction of a magnetic field. Typically used by paranormal researchers to detect a ghost's magnetic energy.

ENTITY - A conscious, interactive ghost. Any being, including people and ghosts.

EXTRASENSORY PERCEPTION (ESP) - The knowledge of external objects or events without the aid of senses.

EXORCISM - The act of ridding a person or a location of demons/evil spirits by using religious rites.

EXORCIST - A person who performs the ridding of demons or other supernatural beings who are alleged to have possessed a person, or (sometimes) a building or even an object.

FALSE AWAKENING - Event in which a person believes they are awake but are actually dreaming.

FEAR CAGE - An area of high EMF readings that can bring out feelings of uneasiness, anxiety and fear.

GAUSS - Is the centimeter-gram-second (CGS) of a magnetic field, which is also known as the "magnetic flux density" or the "magnetic induction."

GHOST - The soul of a deceased person or animal that can appear in visible form or other manifestations to the living. They have not gone through the light, and are stuck between the physical world and the afterlife.

GHOST BOX - A two-way communication device used for communicating with spirits/ghosts.

GHOST HUNTER - One who seeks to experience and document paranormal activity.

GHOST LIGHTS - Strange balls of light that appear in specific locations, often for an extended period of time.

GHOUL - Demonic or parasitic entity that feeds on human remains.

HALLUCINATION - Vivid perception of sights and/or sounds that are not physically present. Usually associated with an altered state of consciousness induced by alcohol, drugs, illness or psychological instability.

HARBINGER - A ghost of the future that brings warnings of impending events.

HAUNTING - Repeated manifestations of unexplained phenomenon that occur at a particular location.

HELLHOUND - Spectral death omen in the form of a ghostly dog.

HOT SPOT - An area within a haunted location where the activity is prominent and/or energy fields are focused.

ILLUSION - A perception between what is perceived and what is reality.

IMPRINT - Events, energy and strong feelings or emotions that are left on an object, a location or even a specific person.

INCUBUS - A demon in male form who, according to a number of mythological and legendary traditions, lies upon sleepers, especially women, in order to have sex with them.

INFESTATION - See Possession.

INSTRUMENTAL TRANS-COMMUNICATION (ITC) - ITC is simply the use of modern electronic devices in an attempt to communicate with spirits. Can be attempted on radios, televisions, computers, telephones and audio recorders.

INTELLIGENT HAUNTING - A haunting by an intelligent or conscious spirit that interacts with living persons.

INVESTIGATION - Carefully controlled research project in which various methods and equipment are used to seek confirmation of reports of ghosts and hauntings.

LEVITATION - To lift or raise a physical object in apparent defiance of gravity.

LIVING APPARITION - The manifestation of an image of a living person that appears in a different location.

LUCID DREAM - A dream in which one is aware they are dreaming.

MALEVOLENT SPIRIT - A spirit who has ill intent.

MANIFESTATION - See Possession.

MATERIALIZATION - The act of forming something solid from air.

MATRIXING - The phenomenon of the mind to complete a picture that is not there.

MEDIUM - A person with the gift of communicating with the dead.

METAPHYSICS - The field of study of phenomenon that is best described as being beyond the laws of physics.

MILLIGAUSS - One thousandth of a gauss.

NATURAL - A rare phenomenon that appears ghostly, but in fact is created by some scientifically unknown property of the present nature.

NEAR-DEATH EXPERIENCE - Experiences of people who have been pronounced medically dead or very close to death.

NECROMANCY - Interacting with the dead, particularly for the purpose of communication or resurrection.

NEGATIVE ENTITY - Inhuman entity, demonic in nature.

NONHUMAN ENTITY - An entity that was never a human on earth. Consists of angels and demons.

OLD HAG SYNDROME - A sleep phenomena that involves a feeling of immobilization, suffocation, odd smells and feelings, and is sometimes accompanied by immense fear.

OPPRESSION - See Possession.

ORBS - Round "lights" caught on film (still or video) that are believed by some to be related to paranormal activity. Very controversial. Most appear to be dust, bugs or moisture.

OUIJA BOARD - A flat board marked with letters of the alphabet, the numbers 0-9 and the words yes, no and goodbye. The Ouija board can supposedly be used to communicate with spirits of the dead. NOTE: IT IS BELIEVED BY SOME THAT THE OUIJA BOARD CAN UNKNOWINGLY INVITE DEMONS/EVIL SPIRITS INTO THE HOME.

OUT-OF-BODY EXPERIENCE - When one's consciousness exits the restrictions of the physical body.

PARANORMAL - Anything beyond what is normal.

PARANORMAL RESEARCH - The study of phenomenon currently considered unexplainable by mainstream sciences.

PARAPSYCHOLOGY - The study of mental abilities and effects outside the usual realm of psychology. Parapsychology includes the study of ESP, ghosts, luck, psychokinesis and other paranormal phenomena.

PAREIDOLIA - The phenomenon when faces and /or shapes are often reported in objects such as doors, trees, clouds, bushes, food and even animals. This is usually nothing paranormal, but a trick of the mind.

PENDULUM - A small weight at the end of a cord or chain that is usually about six to ten inches long. The movement of the weight, when uninfluenced by other factors, can be used to detect areas of paranormal energy.

PHANTOM - Another name for a ghost or spirit. Many use the term to refer to ghosts that have been seen wearing robes or cloaks.

POLTERGEIST - German for "noisy ghost," usually associated with knocking or movement of objects, which often involves an agent.

PORTAL - A theoretical doorway of energy through which spirits may be able to enter or exit a location.

PORTENT - Something that foreshadows a coming event; omen, sign.

POSSESSION - The entry of a spirit into the body of a willing or unwilling host, in which the spirit takes control of the individual's motor and cognitive functions. There are anywhere from three to five stages of possession. Here are four of them:
> Manifestation - Is when the entity is invited in, intentionally or unintentionally.
> Infestation - Is when the entity makes itself known to you. You may have the feeling of being watched; scratching or knocking on the walls, whispers and other paranormal activity.
> Oppression - One of their favorite tactics is to weaken your will by making it difficult for you to sleep. They will also expose any weaknesses, fears, guilt or grief, and use them as a trigger.
> Possession - Is when your active free will has been breached and the entity has access to your body.

PRECOGNITION - Seeing or knowing activity received from the future using ESP.

PREMONITION - A psychic awareness of future events, often with a negative outcome.

PSI - A general term for parapsychological phenomenon.

PSYCHIC - A person who is sensitive beyond the normal means. May be able to see and hear things that are not available to most people.

PSYCHOKINESIS - To move something with the powers of one's mind. Usually associated with poltergeist activity.

RECIPROCAL APPARITION - A rare type of ghost sighting when both the spirit and the human witness see and respond to one another.

RESIDUAL HAUNTING - A repeated haunting in which no intelligent entity or spirit is directly involved. This is the playback of a past event trapped in a continuous loop. It is often associated with past events involving great trauma or tragedy.

RETROCOGNITION - Seeing or knowing activity from the past using ESP.

SÉANCE - A meeting of individuals in order to contact the spirit of a deceased loved one or other person (usually consisting of a medium, assistants, loved ones of the departed or other interested individuals).

SENSITIVE - A person who professes an ability to perceive information through extrasensory perception (ESP).

SHADOW PERSON - A dark fleeting entity seen out of the corner of the eye.

SMUDGING – A cleansing technique with Native American roots where a dried herb bundle or sweetgrass is burned for purification.

SOUL - A soul, in certain spiritual, philosophical and psychological traditions, is the corporeal essence of a person, living thing or object.

SPECTER - Another term for a ghost.

SPIRIT - The actual consciousness or soul of an individual that has passed on, and continues to be observed in an area. They have actually gone through the light, but are able to come and go between the physical world and the afterlife.

SPIRIT ATTACHMENT - When a spirit attaches itself to another person or inanimate object.

SPIRIT REALM - World inhabited by spirits.

SPIRITUALISM - The belief system that the dead are able to communicate with the living, most often through an intermediary or medium.

SUBJECTIVE APPARITION - Hallucination of apparitions or other phenomenon that are created by our own minds.

SUCCUBUS - A female demon appearing in dreams, who takes the form of a human woman in order to seduce men, usually through sexual intercourse.

SUPERNATURAL - Events or happenings that take place in violation of the laws of nature, usually associated with ghosts and hauntings.

TELEKINESIS - The ability to control one's physical environment without using physical manipulation or force (also known as psychokinesis, TK or PK). Usually associated with poltergeist activity.

TELEPATHY - The process by which the mind can communicate directly with another without using normal physical interaction or ordinary sensory perception.

TELEPORTATION - A method of transportation in which matter or information is dematerialized, usually instantaneously, at one point and recreated at another.

VORTEX - The center of paranormal activity thought to be an actual portal to the spirit realm.

WANDERING SPIRIT - A spirit who wanders and briefly stays at a location until their curiosity abates.

WARP - A location where the known laws of physics do not always apply, and space/time may be distorted.

WHITE NOISE - A sound, such as running water, which masks all speech sounds. Used in collection of EVPs.

WRAITH - An apparition of a living person that appears as a portent just before that person's death.

Appendix II

PARANORMAL MOVIES

The following is a list of movies dealing with the paranormal, ghosts, the supernatural, possession and haunted houses, including the year they were released. The list is not all inclusive because I am sure I missed numerous movies that would fit into any one of those categories. You may also find one or two movies listed that do not fit. If so, or if you have a movie to add, please email me at gefeketik@gmail.com.

7 Nights of Darkness	2011
13 Ghosts	1960
100 Feet	2008
1408	2007
2001 Maniacs	2005
A Christmas Carol	2004
A Christmas Carol	2006
A Christmas Carol	2009
A Guy Named Joe	1943
A Haunted House	2013
A Haunted House 2	2014
A Haunting at Silver Falls	2013
A Haunting We Will Go	1942
A Nightmare on Elm Street	1984
A Nightmare on Elm Street 2: Freddy's Revenge	1985
A Nightmare on Elm Street 3: Dream Warriors	1987

Conjuring 2: The Enfield Poltergeist	2016
Coraline	2009
Corpse Bride	2005
The Curse of the Crying Woman	1961
Dark Water	2002
Dark Water	2005
Darkness	2002
Darkness Falls	2003
Dead of Night	1945
Dead Silence	2007
Death Becomes Her	1992
Death of a Ghost Hunter	2007
The Devil's Backbone	2001
The Devil's Rain	1975
Don't be Afraid of the Dark	1973
Don't be Afraid of the Dark	2010
Don't Take It to Heart	1944
Drag Me to Hell	2009
The Echo	2008
The Entity	1981
The Exorcism of Emily Rose	2005
The Exorcist	1973
The Eye	2002
The Eye	2008
The Eye 2	2004
The Eye 10	2005
The Fog	1980
The Fog	2005
FeardotCom	2002
Freddy's Dead: The Final Nightmare	1994
Freddy vs. Jason	2003

The Frighteners	1996
Ghost	1990
The Ghost and Mrs. Muir	1947
The Ghost Breakers	1940
Ghostbusters	1984
Ghostbusters II	1989
The Ghost of Berkeley Square	1947
Ghost Chasers	1951
Ghost Dad	1990
The Ghost Goes West	1936
Ghost in the Machine	1993
The Ghosts of Edendale	2004
Ghost Rider	2006
Ghost Ship	2002
Ghost Story	1981
The Ghost Talks	1949
Ghost Town	2008
The Ghost Walks	1934
Ghosts of Mars	2001
Gildersleeve's Ghost	1944
The Gift	2000
The Gourmet	1984
Gothika	2003
Grave Encounters	2011
The Gravedancers	2006
Grave Secrets: The Legacy of Hilltop Drive	1992
The Grudge	2004
The Grudge 2	2006
The Grudge 3	2009
The Halloween Tree	1993
Haunted	1995

Lady in White	1988
Lani Loa - The Passage	1998
Legend of Hell House	1973
Lonesome Ghost	1937
The Lovely Bones	2009
The Maid	2005
Mama	2013
Maxie	1985
The Messengers	2007
Mirrors	2008
Mirrors 2	2010
Mostly Ghostly: Have You Met My Ghoulfriend?	2014
Mostly Ghostly: Who Let the Ghosts Out?	2008
Nang Nak	1999
The Nightmare Before Christmas	1993
Night of Dark Shadows	1971
Nomads	1986
Oculus	2013
The Old Dark House	1963
Old Mother Riley's Ghosts	1941
The Orphanage	2007
The Other	1972
The Other Side of the Tracks	2008
The Others	2001
Ouija	2014
Over Her Dead Body	2008
Pandora and the Flying Dutchman	1951
Paranormal Activity	2007
Paranormal Activity 2	2010
Paranormal Activity 3	2011
Paranormal Activity 4	2012

Paranormal Activity: The Marked Ones	2014
ParaNorman	2012
Poltergeist	1982
Poltergeist	2015
Poltergeist II	1986
Poltergeist III	1988
Portrait of Jennie	1948
Practical Magic	1998
The Presence	2010
Pulse	2006
Return to House on Haunted Hill	2007
Riding the Bullet	2004
The Ring	2002
The Ring Two	2005
Ringu	1998
Ringu 2	1999
Rinne	2006
R.I.P.D	2013
Route 666	2001
Saint Ange	2004
Scared Stiff	1953
Scary Movie 2	2001
Scary Movie 3	2003
Scary Movie 4	2006
Scary Movie 5	2013
Schalcken the Painter	1979
School Spirit	1985
Scooby Doo	2002
Scooby Doo 2: Monsters Unleashed	2004
The Screaming Skull	1958
Scrooge	1913

Scrooge	1935
Scrooge	1951
Scrooged	1988
Session 9	2001
The Shining	1980
Shock	2004
Shutter	2008
Silent Hill	2006
Silent Tongue	1993
The Sixth Man	1997
The Sixth Sense	1999
The Skeleton Key	2005
Sleepy Hollow	1999
The Smiling Ghost	1941
Someone Behind You	2007
Soul Survivors	2001
The Spirit is Willing	1967
Spook Busters	1946
Stay Alive	2006
Stir of Echoes	1999
Stir of Echoes 2: The Homecoming	2007
Street Trash	1999
Susie Q	1996
Suspiria	1977
Tales of Terror	1962
The Terror	1963
The Time of Their Lives	1946
Thirteen Ghosts	2001
Topper	1937
Topper Returns	1941
Topper Takes a Trip	1938
Tormented	1960
Tormented	2009
Tower of Terror	1997
Trick or Treat	1986
Truly, Madly, Deeply	1990

Appendix III

PARANORMAL TELEVISION SHOWS[49]

The following are television shows that have aired over the years. Included in this list are shows about the paranormal, ghosts, psychics, UFOs, the supernatural, cryptids, history and just about anything else you can think of that deals with the unknown.

Some of these shows were, and are still, very popular. Others barely lasted one season, but as you can see, we have always been fascinated with the unknown. Just like the movie listings, this list may be incomplete also. If you find a show that should be on this list, please email me at gefeketik@gmail.com.

This list was compiled by Sharon A. Hill and used with her permission. Please visit her website, "Doubtful, The Practical Skeptic" at www.idoubtit.wordpress.com.

1949-1950	Ripley's Believe It or Not
1982-1986	
1999	
1959-1961	One Step Beyond (Alcoa Presents…)
1976-1982	In Search Of…
1977-1980	Beyond Reason
1978-1979	The Next Step Beyond
1980	Arthur C. Clarke's Mysterious World
1985	Arthur C. Clarke's World of Strange Powers
1987, 2001	Unsolved Mysteries
1991	James Randi: Psychic Investigator
1991-1995	Haunted Lives/Real Ghosts
1992-1993	Mysteries from Beyond the Other Dominion
1992-1997	Sightings

1993-1996	The Extraordinary
1993-1997	Strange But True?
1994	Arthur C. Clarke's Mysterious Universe
1994	Encounters: The Hidden Truth
1994-1998	Ancient Mysteries
1994-2006	Histories Mysteries
1996	Ghosthunters
1996	Strange Universe
1996-1997	The Paranormal Borderline
1996-2000	Psi Factor: Chronicles of the Paranormal
1996-2000	The Unexplained
1997-1998	Fortean TV
1997-2002	Animal X
1997-2002	Beyond Belief: Fact or Fiction
1998-2008	Haunted History
1999	Exploring the Unknown
1999	The X Creatures
1999-2004	Crossing Over with John Edward
2000-2001	Real Scary Stories
2000-2002	Encounters with the Unexplained
2000-2004	Scariest Places on Earth
2000-2002	MTV's Fear
2001	Ghostwatch Live
2001	Out There TV
2001	Scary…But True
2001-2003	Truth or Scare
2001	Haunted Hotels (America's)
2002	6ixth Sense with Colin Fry
2002	Critical Eye
2002	Most Haunted Live!
2002	Scream Team
2002-2003	Beyond with James Van Praagh
2002-2004	Big Urban Myth
2002-2004	Pet Psychic
2002-2006	Mystery Hunters
2002-2007	Mysterious Journeys

2002-2009	Scared! (On Staten Island)
2002-2006	Creepy Canada
2002-2010	Most Haunted!
2003	The Antiques Ghost Show
2003-2010	Penn & Teller's Bullshit
2003	Unexplained Mysteries
2003-2004	Jane Goldman Investigates
2003-2006	Weird Travels
2004	Proof Positive: Evidence of the Paranormal
2004	Mysterious Encounters
2004	Psychic Detective with Tony Stockwell
2004-2005	I'm Famous and Frightened!
2004-2005	Weird U.S.
2004-2006	Dead Famous
2004-2007	Psychic Detectives
2004-2007	UFO Files
2004-Current	Ghost Hunters
2005	America's Haunted Castles
2005	Derek Acorah's Ghost Towns
2005	Dead Tenants
2005	Enigma
2005	The Girly Ghosthunters
2005	Haunted Houses: Tortured Souls & Restless Spirits
2005	Paranormal?
2005-2006	Psychic Witness
2005-Current	A Haunting
2005-2007	Beyond
2005-2007	Is it Real?
2005-2008	Haunting Evidence
2005-2010	Ghost Whisperer
2005-2011	Ghostly Encounters
2006	Celebrity Paranormal Project
2006	Haunted Homes
2006	Haunted Lighthouses of America
2006	SciFi Investigates

2006	5th Dimension: Secrets of the Supernatural
2006	Unexplained Canada
2006-2007	Extreme Ghost Stories
2006-2008	Ghost Trackers
2006-2009	Psychic Investigators
2006-2010	Ghosthunting with...
2006-2010	Rescue Mediums
2006-2011	Paranormal State
2007	America's Psychic Challenge
2007	Investigations of the Unexplained
2007	Phenomenon/The Successor
2007-2008	Spook School Unexplained
2007-2010	Monster Quest
2007-2014	Destination Truth
2008-2012	Ghost Hunters International
2007-2008,	The Real Exorcist (Bob Larson)
2008	Paranormal Egypt
2008, 2011	The One
2008	The Unexplained with George Noory
2008-2009	Living with the Dead
2008-2009	UFO Hunters
2008-Current	Ghost Adventures
2009	Extreme Paranormal
2009	Ghost Cases
2009	Ghost Hunters Academy
2009	Ghost Intervention
2009	The Haunted
2009	Nostradamus Effect
2009	The Othersiders
2009-2010	Ghost Stories
2009-2010	Most Terrifying Places in America
2009-2011	Ghost Lab
2009-2011	Conspiracy Theory w/Jesse Ventura
2009-2013	Celebrity Ghost Stories
2009	Mystery Quest
2009-2011	Psychic Kids

2009-Current	River Monsters
2010-2012	Fact or Faked: Paranormal Files
2010	American Paranormal
2010	Real and Chance: The Legend Hunters
2010-2011	Ancient X Files
2010	Derren Brown Investigates
2010	Freak Encounters
2010	Mary Knows Best
2010	Paranatural
2010	Paranormal Cops
2010	Pet Psychic Encounters
2010	Weird or What
2010	My Ghost Story
2010-Current	Ancient Aliens
2010	Brad Meltzer's Decoded
2010	Paranormal State: The New Class
2010-Current	Mysteries at the Museum
2011	Beast Hunter
2011	I Survived…Beyond and Back
2011	Miracle Detectives
2011-2012	Paranormal Home Inspectors
2011-Current	Finding Bigfoot
2011-2013	Haunted Collector
2011	Legend Quest
2011	From Beyond
2011	Paranormal Witness
2011	Long Island Medium
2011	Celebrity Ghost Hunt
2011	Dark Matters: Twisted but True
2011	The Truth Beyond…
2011	Paranormal Challenge
2011-Current	The Dead Files
2012	The Exorcist Files
2012	Beyond Belief
2012	School Spirits
2012	Countdown to the Apocalypse

2012-2013	Haunted Highway
2012-2013	Ghost Mine
2012	Chasing UFOs
2012	Conspiracy Road Trip
2012	Professor Weird
2012	Paranormal Paparazzi
2012	Cursed
2012	UFOs: The Untold Stories
2012	Haunted Encounters: Face to Face
2012	Unsealed: Conspiracy Files
2012	Unsealed: Alien Files
2012-Current	The Haunting Of…
2013	Stranded
2013-2014	Deep South Paranormal
2013	Alien Mysteries
2013	Monsters and Mysteries in America
2013	Killer Contact
2013	Joe Rogan Questions Everything
2013	Psychic Tia
2013	The Unexplained Files
2013	Stalked by a Ghost
2013	Ghost Inside My Child
2013	Ghost Bait
2013	Mountain Monsters
2013	When Ghosts Attack
2013	The Monster Project
2013	Mystery Map
2013	The Curse of Oak Island
2013	America's Book of Secrets
2013-Current	My Haunted House
2014	Haunting: Australia
2014	10 Million Dollar Big Foot Bounty
2014	Cryptid: The Swamp Beast
2014	Hangar 1: The UFO Files
2014	Cell Block Psychic
2014	The R.I.P. Files

Appendix IV

PHOTO CREDITS

Front Cover - Designed by Greg Feketik. Ohio Cottage and the "Doll" used with the permission of Madison Seminary

Figure 1 - Photograph used with permission of the Milne Special Collections, University of New Hampshire Library, Durham, NH

Figure 2 - Photograph used with permission of the Milne Special Collections, University of New Hampshire Library, Durham, NH

Figure 3 - Photograph courtesy of the Naval Air Station Ft. Lauderdale Museum, Ft. Lauderdale, FL, www.nasflmuseum.com

Figure 4 - Photograph in the public domain, courtesy of www.worldwar2headquarters.com

Figure 5 - Drawing in the public domain. Courtesy of www.wikimedia.org

Figure 6 - Photograph used under the terms of the GNU Free Documentation License Version 1.2. Courtesy of Author Versageek, www.wikimedia.org. This photograph was changed from color to B&W.

Figure 7 - Photograph used under the terms of the Creative Commons Attribution - Share Alike 3.0. Courtesy of Author BrownieCharles99, www.wikimedia.org. No changes were made to this photograph.

Figure 8 - Photograph by Greg Feketik

Figure 9 - Photograph by Greg Feketik

Figure 10 - Photograph by Greg Feketik

Figure 11 - Photograph by Greg Feketik

Figure 12 - Photograph by Greg Feketik

Figure 13 - Photograph by Greg Feketik. Used with permission of Carriage Tours of Savannah, www.carriagetoursofsavannah.com

Figure 14 - Photograph by Greg Feketik. Used with permission of the Marshall House Hotel, www.marshallhouse.com

Figure 15 - Photograph by Greg Feketik

Figure 16 - Photograph by Greg Feketik. Used with permission of Wakely Properties, LLC

Figure 17 - Photograph by Greg Feketik. Used with permission of Wakely Properties, LLC

Figure 18 - Photograph by Greg Feketik. Used with permission of the Buxton Inn, www.buxtoninn.com

Figure 19 - Photograph by Greg Feketik. Used with permission of the Buxton Inn, www.buxtoninn.com

Figure 20 - Photograph by Greg Feketik. Used with permission of the Buxton Inn, www.buxtoninn.com

Figure 21 - Photograph by Greg Feketik. Used with permission of the Buxton Inn, www.buxtoninn.com

Figure 22 - Photograph by Greg Feketik. Used with permission of the Buxton Inn, www.buxtoninn.com

Figure 23 - Photograph courtesy of the Buxton Inn, www.buxtoninn.com

Figure 24 - Photograph courtesy of the Buxton Inn, www.buxtoninn.com

Figure 25 - Photograph by Greg Feketik. Used with permission from the homeowner

Figure 26 - Photograph by Greg Feketik. Used with permission from the homeowner

Figure 27 - Photograph by Greg Feketik. Used with permission of the Ohio State Reformatory, www.mrps.org

Figure 28 - Photograph by Greg Feketik. Used with permission of the Ohio State Reformatory, www.mrps.org

Figure 29 - Photograph by Greg Feketik. Used with permission of the Ohio State Reformatory, www.mrps.org

Figure 30 - Photograph by Greg Feketik. Used with permission of the Ohio State Reformatory, www.mrps.org

Figure 31 - Photograph by Greg Feketik. Used with permission of Madison Seminary

Figure 32 - Photograph by Greg Feketik. Used with permission of Madison Seminary

Figure 33 - Photograph by Greg Feketik. Used with permission of Madison Seminary

Figure 34 - Photograph by Greg Feketik. Used with permission of Madison Seminary

Figure 35 - Photograph by Greg Feketik. Used with permission of Madison Seminary

Figure 36 - Photograph by Greg Feketik. Used with permission of Madison Seminary

Figure 37 - Photograph by Greg Feketik. Used with permission of Madison Seminary

Figure 38 - Photograph by Greg Feketik. Used with permission of Madison Seminary

Figure 39 - Photograph by Greg Feketik. Used with permission of Madison Seminary

Figure 40 - Photograph by Greg Feketik. Used with permission of Prospect Place, www.gwacenter.org

Figure 41 - Photograph by Greg Feketik. Used with permission of Prospect Place, www.gwacenter.org

Figure 42 - Photograph by Greg Feketik. Used with permission of Prospect Place, www.gwacenter.org

Figure 43 - Photograph by Steven Hillegass. Used with permission of Prospect Place, www.gwacenter.org

Figure 44 - Photograph by Greg Feketik. Used with permission of Prospect Place, www.gwacenter.org

Figure 45 - Photograph by Steven Hillegass. Used with permission of Prospect Place, www.gwacenter.org

Figure 46 - Photograph by Greg Feketik

Figure 47 - Photograph by Greg Feketik

Appendix V

REFERENCES/END NOTES

[1] www.amazon.com/The-Art-Science-Paranormal-Investigation/dp/1466265884

[2] en.wikipedia.org/wiki/Twinsburg,_Ohio

[3] www.clevelandmemory.org/press

[4] en.wikipedia.org/wiki/Ball_lightning

[5] www.thrillingdetective.com/3investigators.html

[6] www.hardyboys.us

[7] www.stateofhorror.com/momo.html

[8] www.jacobite.co.uk

[9] www.slappedham.com/betty-barney-hill-alien-abduction

[10] www.nasflmuseum.com

[11] www.mysteriousuniverse.org/2014/07/the-mysterious- moving-coffins-of-barbados

[12] www.imdb.com/title/tt0077610

[13] www.sites.google.com/site/eastern401

[14] www.amazon.com/The-Amityville-Horror-Jay-Anson/dp/1416507698

[15] www.biography.com/people/ronald-defeo-580972

[16] www.moberlymo.org

[17] www.gawker.com/how-the-ouija-board-became-the-mouthpiece-of-the-devil-1456245561

[18] www.savannah.com

[19] www.carriagetoursofsavannah.com

[20] www.marshallhouse.com

[21] www.historynet.com/minie-ball

[22] www.murderpedia.org/female.R/r/riley-alice.htm

[23] www.visit-historic-savannah.com/colonial-park-cemetery.html

[24] www.phrases.org.uk/meanings/saved-by-the-bell.html

[25] www.juliettegordonlowbirthplace.org

[26] www.buxtoninn.com

[27] www.cashtowninn.com

[28] www.ridersinn.com

[29] en.wikipedia.org/wiki/Parma,_Ohio

[30] www.emfcenter.com/emffaqs.htm

[31] www.mrps.org

[32] www.facebook.com/pages/Madison-Seminary/180590777832

[33] www.rootsweb.ancestry.com/~ohlake/institutions/cotbarhx

[34] en.wikipedia.org/wiki/Haunted_Collector

[35] www.imdb.com/title/tt2072029

[36] www.gwacenter.org

[37] www.imdb.com/title/tt0069992

[38] www.imdb.com/title/tt0073820

[39] en.wikipedia.org/wiki/In_Search_of..._(TV_series)

[40] www.biography.com/people/leonard-nimoy-9423757

[41] en.wikipedia.org/wiki/Scooby-Doo,_Where_Are_You!

[42] www.slashfilm.com/watch-audiences-react-to-the-exorcist-in-vintage-1973-footage

[43] www.snopes.com/language/literary/dracula.asp

[44] en.wikipedia.org/wiki/Werewolf#Vulnerabilities

[45] www.bramstoker.org

[46] www.nosferatumovie.com

[47] www.therealwaverlyhills.com

[48] www.farnsworthhouseinn.com

[49] www.idoubtit.wordpress.com/paranormaltv

Made in the USA
Lexington, KY
30 August 2016